ROBIN STUBBS has practised as a craft jeweller for the past 12 years and is highly regarded in her profession. She studied with W. van Heeckereen at the School for Silversmiths in Sydney. Robin has been a catalyst in bringing together jewellers in New South Wales and helping to organize the New South Wales Jewellers Group and from 1980 to 1984 she was the State Representative of the Jewellers and Metalsmiths Group of Australia. In 1982 Robin was the organiser of the workshops for women jewellers which were run during the 'Women in the Arts' festival in New South Wales. The enthusiasm that these generated was continued in the 'Worn Issues' exhibitions and workshops which Robin has been involved in from 1983 to the present. As well as jewellery, her interests extend to many other crafts and she has been on the committee of the Crafts Council of New South Wales, and attended the international conferences of the World Craft Council in Kyoto and Vienna.

THE
SUPPORT
YOURSELF
SERIES

JEWELLERY

Robin Stubbs

FONTANA/COLLINS

© Robin Stubbs, 1986

First published in 1986 by Fontana Books (the paperback
imprint of William Collins Pty Ltd), Sydney.

Typeset by Post Typesetters, Brisbane
Printed and bound by Globe Press, Melbourne

National Library of Australia
Cataloguing-in-Publication data:

Stubbs, Robin.
  Jewellery.

  Bibliography.

  ISBN 0 00 636576 0.

1. Jewellery making. I. Title.
(Series: The support yourself series).

739.27

I have always believed I could do anything if I was determined enough. Writing a book has been quite a test of that philosophy. I could not have achieved it without the support of my family and friends.

I would like to specially thank Jenny Ioynbee Wilson for her encouragement. Jewellers were generous sharing their experiences and knowledge and I would like to thank all of you for your friendship and interest.

CONTENTS

INTRODUCTION

T HAT'S an unusual piece of jewellery you're wearing,' says a stranger at a party and before you can reply, a friend will offer, 'Robin is a jeweller, she probably made it herself.' A whole barrage of questions follows culminating in the remark, 'What an interesting hobby.'

If you then think, 'No, it's not a hobby—it's something more. It is my craft, my main interest, my life, something I need to do every day,' then this book can help you. Sometimes a trigger situation like the one described can make you review just where you're at.

Perhaps you know nothing at all about how jewellery is made but think it's an interesting craft and you'd like to find out more about it. This book is for the enthusiastic beginner to show just how broad the subject of jewellery can be and how it can lead to a rewarding career.

Or maybe you yourself have been dissatisfied lately with the quality of your craft work even though the pieces are technically sound, the designs pleasing and friends and charities want your work. There are probably family pressures, too, so you cannot give your craft as much time as you would like. Instead of feeling happy with your work you feel frustrated and fragmented. You know why the problem exists but not how to fix it. These are positive feelings, so make use of them. They are all strong signs pointing to the fact that you are ready for an exciting change.

This book can be used in many ways:

- As a guide for the beginner
- As an information source for the leisure-time jeweller
- As a stimulus to help you move from being a hobbyist to becoming a part-time jeweller
- As a checklist to establish your level of professionalism.

Guidelines

Anyone can do anything if they are interested and determined. For the *beginner* who has admired skill in other people's craft, let this book put you on the right track. The Appendix, with information on where to learn, books to read and organizations to contact, is your jumping-off point.

While it's possible to explore by yourself some of the processes in the recommended books, it is still advantageous for beginners to find classes to attend. Even though quite a few people have managed to become self-taught jewellers, classes help to encourage enthusiasm and curiosity and keenness to get ahead and learn quickly. Classes discourage the cultivation of incorrect or time-consuming habits and your progress will be logical.

Information

If you have been making jewellery in your *leisure* time and enjoy it but feel you would like to know more, there are many helpful suggestions in this book. When you want to keep your craft time at the level it is now and still sell some work and occasionally exhibit, use the chapters on pricing and presentation to help you. There is no reason for the work or your approach to be amateurish just because jewellery-making is a leisure-time occupation.

Stimulus

Quite a few of the jewellers whose work is represented in Australian collections started making jewellery as a *hobby*. It soon became an overriding interest, part of their lifestyle, and something that changed and enriched their lives. You, too, can make this exciting change. Obviously, you have the interest and with just a little step you can make the commitment to becoming a part-time jeweller. By using the self-assessment sections in Chapter 1 you can review your work and attitudes and may find you are closer to becoming a part-time jeweller than you thought. If you are selling some jewellery now, your problem could involve a plan to increase volume. Step-by-step planning and its details are in Chapter 4.

Checklist

When you have sold some of your work, use the information in this book to check that you are being *pro-*

and some, by their makers' standards, are precious. The New Guinea kina made from one large shell and worn as a breast plate, as well as being a symbol of rank, looks stunning. The finely woven armbands, the feathered headdresses and the irridescent beetle headbands are all possible sources of inspiration and stimulus.

People have always decorated themselves using jewellery as a status symbol or as a form of saving. We have not changed. Men, as well as women, are wearing more and more jewellery. As economic conditions get tighter, it seems we make ourselves look brighter, more colourful, sparkling and noticeable.

The Australian Background to Jewellery

In Australia, jewellery and silversmithing is a reflection of our social and economic history. From our early convict beginnings through the gold rush of the 1850s and 1860s, to the extravagance of the late 1890s and the developing manufacturing industries in the early 1900s, there developed a style peculiar to Australian silversmithing.

Our earliest goldsmiths and silversmiths were convicts and their work was plain, almost stark in design, reflecting the life style of the first settlers. With immigration and the growth of the colony in the early 1800s, more silversmiths arrived. As early as 1803 the first advertisement by W. Moreton, watchmaker, goldsmith and jeweller appeared in the *Sydney Gazette* of 15 May.

In 1813 in his proclamation of 28 June Governor Macquarie ordered:

... that from and After the said 30th day of September No Person shall practice or Exercise within this Territory the art Trade or Mystery of a Working Jeweller or Goldsmith, unless he shall first bind himself to the Superintendant of Police in the Town of Sydney in the penal Sum of One Hundred Pounds, and two Sufficient Sureties in the Sum of Fifty Pounds each, not to forge, make, falsify, Counterfeit, Melt down, Impair, diminish, scale or lighten any of the Silver money hereby Allowed to be Current in this Territory ...

No doubt he was concerned about the changeover from rum to coin as the colony's currency!

One of these early silversmiths, Alexander Dick, a free settler, noted for his racing trophies and flatware, was indicted in 1829 for receiving twelve dessertspoons stolen from the residence of the Colonial Secretary, Alexander Macleay, and sentenced to seven years transportation to Norfolk Island. Perhaps Mr Dick was short of materials that year.

The discovery of gold in New South Wales in 1851 and shortly afterwards in Victoria, as well as silver at Broken Hill, led to a rapid increase in the population as immigrants dashed to the gold-fields. Some of the earliest and most unusual pieces of Australian jewellery date from this time. These are gold-field brooches with designs of miniature picks, shovels, gold pans and sieves decorated with gold nuggets or gold quartz.

During the gold rush many goldsmiths and silversmiths migrated to Australia. These first silversmiths, most of them qualified and experienced, were responsible for establishing the retail trade in Sydney, Melbourne and Adelaide. There was little contact between the States because of distance, communication and travel difficulties. Because of these difficulties and the influence of migrants from different countries, the style of work from each State varied, with Adelaide as an example, showing a strong German influence.

A new period in Australian silver developed from about 1840 to 1890, depending on the State where it was made. Colonial silver was extravagant, opulent and over-decorated with kangaroos, emus, Aborigines, flowers and ferns and all possible Australiana. Emu eggs were carved, mounted, lined, or covered, and used in every conceivable way. Leading silversmiths at this time were William Edwards in Melbourne, Henry Steiner in Adelaide and Evan Jones in Sydney and their work is typical of that period.

William Edwards arrived in Melbourne in 1857 and was a prolific and distinguished maker of Colonial silver. An example of his work is a scent bottle made from a leather-covered, divided emu egg with handles of flowers and a parakeet, and grapevine tendrils and fruit finial to open the egg.

Henry Steiner arrived in Adelaide in 1858 and he, too, was a most prolific maker of presentation pieces and emu egg extravagances, including the only emu egg candlestick. His tankard made from an emu egg reflects his German tradition.

Evan Jones arrived in Sydney in 1855 and his work included many racing trophies, medals, tea and coffee services decorated with ferns, kangaroos and Aborigines, as well as jewellery and emu egg pieces. His bachelor teapot using an emu egg with a silver emu head spout and mounted on silver clawed feet is an incredible piece.

The National Gallery of Victoria has the fine J. & J. Altmann Collection with pieces dated from 1820 to 1900. In the words of T. Lane, Curator Decorative Arts of the National Gallery in Victoria. It can be said 'to represent the whole range of Australian silver from Alexander Dick's chaste designs for flatware to the most bizarre manifestations of the emu egg craze'.

The early silversmiths worked mainly by commission and this included jewellery and kept very little of what they made in stock. Until the 1880 to 1890 decade, most work was handmade and, in the smaller workshops, continued to be handmade even later than this.

Up to 1900 jewellery and silversmithing flourished. After 1900 it all seemed to fade away to be replaced by imports of mass-produced, conventional precious jewellery which flooded the market. A few arts and crafts jewellers kept the craft tradition alive and among them was Rhoda Wager, an English jeweller who came out to Australia and opened a studio in Rowe Street, Sydney, in 1928. For twenty-five years Rhoda Wager made jewellery, all carefully recorded in her sketch books. Her designs, too, have an Australian theme. Her niece, Dorothy Wager, who trained with her aunt, lives in New South Wales and still makes some of the original designs. Dorothy Wager did not assess the work as very significant or the original sketchbooks as valuable. But how exciting it is for those interested in the history of Australian jewellery to discover such detailed records spanning nearly sixty years!

Great impetus was again given to Australian craft jewellery by the migration of jewellers to Australia during 1950–60. Among those who arrived and greatly influenced the jewellery movement were Wolf Wennrich (1953), Emmanuel Raft (1956), Helge Larsen

(1961, Head of Department, Jewellery and Silversmithing, Sydney College of the Arts), Wal van Heeckeren (1968, first private School for Silversmiths, founded 1969), and Frank Bauer (1972).

These people and their students, plus the growth of the crafts movement in the 1970s are responsible for establishing contemporary jewellery in Australia. (See Margaret Jasulaitis', 'Jewellery in Australia, Historical Notes', Contemporary Australian Jewellery Catalogue, 1979.)

There are now many opportunities to learn how to make jewellery but it wasn't always so. Until the Jewellery School at the Royal Melbourne Institute of Technology was established in 1960 there were no formal courses in jewellery. Craft jewellers were mainly self-taught and they were only few. Trade jewellers provided a limited number of places for apprenticeships of three years together with attendance at a technical college eight hours a week. Places for apprenticeship training are still limited.

In 1970, the first national exhibition of Australian jewellery to be shown overseas, *Australian Jewellery* toured Southeast Asia. In 1980, *Objects To Human Scale* travelled Japan and other Asian countries. In 1982, *Australian Jewellery* toured Europe, exhibiting the widest survey of contemporary Australian jewellery so far. It was exciting to see the work of so many young jewellers from all the States of Australia.

It is pertinent and notable that the materials used by so many contemporary jewellers have moved away from the traditional precious metals. Plastics, fibre, natural materials, paper, rubber, film, paint, steel, lead, copper and brass are some of the materials used. All are readily available and not very expensive.

The environment for making jewellery today is a

stimulating and inspiring one. There is an increasing awareness of craftspeople in the community and the importance of handmade objects. Jewellery is no longer necessarily precious or permanent. Materials are limited only by one's imagination. Opportunities to learn at all levels are available all over Australia. You can take advantage of this positive environment to develop your own individual potential as a jeweller.

You will find throughout this book examples of successful jewellers. Some, like Dorothy Erickson, have carefully planned their careers. Others like Mike Wilson, have made the decision to become a jeweller instantenously. Jewellers who combine their own designs with work made to fit market demands include Marion Marshall and Daniel Jenkins. Some, like Darani Lewers, Helge Larsen and Wal van Heeckeren, have been working many years contributing their knowledge and leading the way for others to follow. Others, like Robyn Gordon, have found a particular material and made it their speciality.

From all of these jewellers we can learn, be inspired and encouraged to travel our own individual path to a successful goal.

Darani Lewers and Helge Larsen

The story of the transition of Darani Lewers and Helge Larsen from master and apprentice in Denmark in 1959 to that of equal partners has been told in Patricia Thompson's book, *Twelve Australian Craftsmen.* Another transition would be the one they made from Denmark to Australia and the major influence their work has had on Australian jewellery.

In 1961, Darani and Helge migrated to Australia and in a very short time they opened a workshop at Circular Quay and began working for an exhibition. This exhibition, at the Macquarie Galleries in 1961, was the first jewellery exhibition held in Sydney and had considerable impact. The organic forms of their jewellery using stones, wood and shell with sterling silver was most unusual for those days. Although a few commissions and an exhibition in Perth followed, survival was not easy. Before the Macquarie exhibition, five pieces were made and selected for the first International Exhibition of Modern Jewellery at the Goldsmiths Hall, London—the only jewellery from Australia to be included.

From 1965 to 1973, Helge lectured in design at the University of New South Wales. Darani would work in the workshop during the day, as well as looking after children and a home. The pace must have been hectic and their production constant as sixteen exhibitions were held between 1961 and 1961. Helge says this time was very pleasant as they 'had a close relationships with clients and talked to them before designing'. Two pieces were often made for the client's choice which left one for an exhibition, and their work was never sold to shops. From 1973 to 1977 they supported themselves entirely from their jewellery.

The early organic pieces and work that was Danish in style was followed by jewellery which considered the body and its natural movement. Between 1973 and 1975 some of their best known jewellery developed which included the acrylic and sterling silver pendants showing the Opera House, the Harbour Bridge and Australian postage stamps. This series used materials different from the precious metals and stones traditionally used in Australian jewellery. 'Something had to happen to break away from established materials', and again Helge and Darani led the way.

In 1977, Helge Larsen established the Jewellery and Silver Smithing Department of the Sydney College of the Arts. Although his position at the College is demanding, he has recently begun to explore the use of relatively inexpensive materials such as stainless steel. He was also the selector for *Objects to Human Scale* which was the first important survey exhibition of contemporary Australian jewellery. During 1976 to 1980, Darani Lewers chaired the meetings of the Crafts Board of the Australia Council, and these years became an important time for the development of craft in Australia. From 1980 to 1984 she lectured on jewellery at the City Art Institute, Sydney, as well as continuing her own work. Her present direction involves ideas-based jewellery—taking a subject, researching it, and making a statement with jewellery. She is interested in working on a variety of levels ranging from inexpensive jewellery made as a series to one-off experimental work.

What do Darani and Helge see happening to jewellery in the future? They agreed that jewellery is taking three different directions. The first approach is the continuation of the tradition of using precious stones and materials. The second approach is concerned with speculative work, making a highly personal statement using a variety of materials. This work tends to be expensive. The third approach focuses on low-cost series and production work which appeals to a wider public. Such an approach requires ingenuity of design and flexibility of approach and materials. This is perhaps the most exciting trend which has the potential for redefining jewellery and making it more accessible to the public.

CHAPTER 1

Starting Points

THIS chapter is for the student who is just beginning to extend himself and for the craft jeweller who finds it a satisfying hobby.

If jewellery is a hobby for you, I know you well. You have been making jewellery for a few years and selling some of it. You still go to classes part-time or for a special project. But making jewellery is taking more and more of your time and now you are wondering if you can make a living from it. The self-assessment in this chapter should help to clarify your thoughts.

If you are a jewellery student, is part-time work helping you survive? Whatever the work may be, in or out of the field of jewellery, you can use it to help your jewellery skills and your selling skills. Your jewellery-making will benefit from searching for inexpensive materials, making something out of nothing; paper, bone, recycled materials, threads, hair, even pieces picked up from the road. Any contacts you may have with the public give you a great opportunity to observe and understand people's attitudes, how they dress, what jewellery is worn, and how money is spent.

These are valuable observations to keep in mind for that time when you are working as a jeweller supplying the public.

You may be one of those rare individuals who decided to become a full-time jeweller, gave up what you were doing and started by working hard at everything at once, not only learning and making but also selling. This is possible with hard work, single mindedness and great optimism. It has been done! Mike Wilson started this way in 1972. (More about him later in this chapter.)

Perhaps you are a well-trained jeweller working part-time, exhibiting and selling but not really making enough money to live on. One skill you may not have learned is marketing. Not many professional craftspeople consider marketing seriously, believing it will restrict their flexibility and creativity. *The Crafts as a Livelihood Project Report,* October, 1979, undertaken by the Crafts Council of Australia, surveyed a group of craftspeople over a two-year period. Some of the reported attitudes included 'a fear of using management techniques', and 'marketing techniques seem too commercial'. The people surveyed were also 'not used to receiving input from outside their own studio'. These attitudes are changing and craftspeople are realizing their need to develop a professional approach to all aspects of their work.

To be independent, work for yourself and earn enough to live on is the dream of many people. To have uncommitted money or a second income, to repay the mortgage loan, extend the house or have a holiday are all goals towards which you can work. Whether student, hobbyist or beginner, the dream can become a reality. How to earn money is just another technique to learn.

Take a hard look at yourself, your time, your attitude to work, your jewellery and business skills and your needs, both short- and long-term. By doing this carefully you are assessing *why* and *how* to be an income-earning jeweller. The answers may indicate that you start on a part-time basis planning to be a full-time jeweller within three years. Whatever the answers are for you, they should help you set goals and develop a plan.

Reasons

Why do you want to earn your living as a jeweller?

- Is it the satisfaction of working with your hands?
- Do you enjoy being creative?
- Does the way of life appeal to you?
- Is it a challenge to be self-employed?
- Do you enjoy both making and selling, the whole process?

Being creative, working with your hands, following the whole idea through to completion is a very personal process. Most artists become attached to their creations. You may need to detach yourself so you can look at pieces from a selling viewpoint. I assume you will be in business to make money, as well as pieces to please yourself. This does not mean compromising the quality or making pieces you dislike. It does mean learning to make an impartial and unemotional judgement about your work, adapting to market demands, choosing designs that can be repeated. Can you make the same piece many times, using one process at a time, to develop a number of similar pieces? For crafts-people already selling individual pieces, it could require a difficult change of attitude.

Being self-employed can mean a complete change in life style and you could feel in time that the business owns you. If you are accustomed to a regular income and regular working hours, can you adjust? To work when and how you choose may be the reasons you want your own business. It can mean a lot of changes which are better looked at now. Perhaps you do not care about the usual status symbol possesions, the conventional attitudes to credit, planning for luxuries, holidays and outings. Are these pressures you want to avoid the very reasons you want to have a business of your own? Give these questions a lot of thought. Have you a partner, a family? Can they adjust too? If you have a partner and will be working as a team, consider whether you can spend twenty-four hours a day together. Some safety valves such as private areas in your house where you can be alone and separate contacts with other people need to be arranged and considered, no matter how compatible the relation-ship. When your workshop is part of your home, you will need to keep it from overflowing into the whole house and your entire life.

Contacting and meeting people, getting out into the market-place is something you would like to do as well as making jewellery. You feel confident and have enjoyed the contact with clients you have had up to now. Can you do it regularly when it is man-datory, whether you feel like it or not? Can you take knockbacks from people who may not like your work? Again, you will need to develop an objective attitude.

If you check through your attitudes to work and decide to be optimistic and that making jewellery and selling it is right for you, then welcome to the happy crowd who have made the same decision.

Self-Assessment

Having made that important decision, do you have the talent and ability to make saleable jewellery? The self-asssessment lists on the following pages will help you answer these questions and decide how many processes you know and how skilful you are in each one. There are various ways to judge your own work. Be realistic but not overcritical.

1 Analyse your work Take several of your pieces and look at them critically. Is the workmanship faultless? Is the finish perfect? Does everything work as it should and does the piece have sales appeal? Evaluate the strong points about your work and why someone would want to buy it. Are you satisfied with these pieces? When looking at a number of items, is there a distinctive style? Make a list of the strong and weak points of your work. If a beginner, do not be depressed if the weak list is longer as you are probably being overcritical.

2 Compare your work Look in shops and jewellers' studios to see what is being sold and how it's made. Can you achieve the same standard and do you have some new ideas? You are possibly aware of what is being sold and this could be one of the reasons you, too, decided to sell jewellery.

3 Rate your work Take a few pieces and mark them on (a) workmanship, (b) originality, (c) function, and (d) sales appeal.

(a) **Workmanship**: Is it technically perfect? A hand-made piece should not look thrown together. There should be no sharp edges, weak joints, loose parts. Square corners should be square, circles round, and the whole piece properly finished.

(b) **Originality**: Have you made different use of materials, not the same as in commercially produced jewellery?

(c) **Function**: The jewellery should sit well on the body, be light enough to wear and fit correctly.

(d) **Sales appeal**: Your work will need to suit a diversity of people, have a wide appeal and be a competitive price.

Using a scale of one to five, mark these different aspects of your work according to the following criteria:

1 Poor
2 Fair
3 Average
4 Good
5 Excellent

Take your rating list and scale of marking to another jeweller. Do not take your own marks. Ask him to rate your work on the same basis. Then compare the two sets of marks, your self-marking and that of the other person. Look for the differences. The trick is not to worry about a difference of one point but to look for variations in the assessment. Be aware that when you mark yourself you will usually indicate a strong tendency to undervalue your ability. If there are big gaps in the assessment you will need to take a close look at those areas. Can the other person see weaknesses in your work? Ask for constructive criticism but do not let it ruin a friendship. Alternatively, seek a third assessment.

4 Exhibitions and collections are valuable reference points Look at a piece which interests you and work out how it was made. Think of your own skill. Would you be able to make that piece? Perhaps you can see a simpler way to make it. No idea how it was made? Why is the piece in a special collection?

When you have compared your work with that of others you will be able to pinpoint your strengths and weaknesses. Write them down and try to spell out the nature of each.

These are four ways to assess your work. Use one or more. It is amazing how much enthusiasm you can generate by a realistic self-assessment. It makes you sure of what you really know and what you are doing. That is a tremendous help to feeling confident in the areas where you are strong. The assessment will also show you what you still need to master.

Another reason to honestly evaluate your work is not only to avoid failure but to make sure you are not putting poor quality work on the market and lowering the standards established by other jewellers.

As a student or hobby jeweller you will probably have sold work. Have you talked to those first customers? Have they come back for another piece? Often you will get worthwhile information from buyers if you ask. If you do not ask and there has been a weakness in the piece, you lose a client. People will avoid telling you out of politeness or annoyance. When you encourage feedback, responses will enable you to gauge consistent problems and successes. Be tactful and interested and you will be surprised how much you will learn.

Processes or Techniques

The definition of technique is 'the means of achieving one's purpose'. Your purpose is to make a variety of saleable jewellery pieces. Therefore, the more techniques you become skilled in, the wider variety of jewellery you can make.

Jewellery is now made from almost any material. However, as processes for nonferrous metal jewellery are what many jewellers learn first, let us check those first. Again, rate yourself one to five for each.

- Shaping processes: sawing, filing, hammering.
- Soldering.
- Fastening processes: rivetting, hinging, for example.
- Finishing processes: emery, polish, burnish.

This is a basic list for you to evaluate your skill. (A complete list of processes is in Chapter 2 for your reference.) Have you found you rate well in only a few? That is a good start. There are many examples of successful people who specialize, doing just a few things well.

I once knew a little old lady, a Mrs James, who made quite a good living from her sterling silver jewellery. Mr James was a retired tradesman who made only sterling silver spoons with gumnut shaped handles. Both Mr and Mrs James had limited knowledge but considerable confidence and self-promotion. Mrs James made fused 'nests' from sterling silver. They were unusual, wearable, and attractive. The strong points were an interesting texture, a varied finish and no untidy sharp ends. Both Mr and Mrs James enjoyed their work and it boosted their pension, gave them an interest and contact with other people. This is a good example of limited skill with few tools and a small workbench but with many benefits.

However, do not stop with one process. While you are selling pieces made only one way, start learning something new and develop your versatility. Who knows when the market may change? Competition is likely from jewellers using many processes to make a wide variety of jewellery. It is important to keep ahead of competitors if you want a share of the market. There have been opportunities in the last few years to attend workshops in special techniques including colouring metals, married metals, textile techniques for jewellers, and plastics. Committed and enthusiastic jewellers are always ready to learn something more.

If you do decide to go in one particular direction, it can be profitable as well as interesting if you extend the materials and yourself. Generally the jeweller who decides to specialize in one area has other training. It is possible to become so interested in one process or material that you keep exploring all possibilities and achieving results that no one realized could be done. In this way the jeweller Barbara Ryman has experimented with stainless steel and laminex. When she was an impecunious student, these cheaper materials enabled Barbara to experiment with colour, shape, different fastenings and eventually to include small inlaid areas of enamelled silver.

You have now looked at why you want to be a self-supporting jeweller and decided you have the talent and enthusiasm. You also need to decide if you have the time and space to achieve this ambition.

Time

How do you use your time now? Whether a student, housewife, breadwinner, or part-time jeweller, we all have regular commitments as well as spare time. Have you enough spare time to make jewellery on a money-making scale? What can be sorted out, left out or rescheduled to give you a large slice of time when you need it? Large amounts of time are necessary for the actual making of jewellery. Little slots of time can be used for some of the related tasks such as buying supplies or calling on retailers. My day starts at 5:30 a.m. from September to December as this gives me at least one and a half hours of uninterrupted time during a busy season. If you are counting on time at night or after work as spare time, remember you need to eat!

The time you have available to put into making jewellery will partly determine how much money you can make. In the beginning you could be working at two occupations: earning enough to live on from your usual job and then working at home to build up stock to move into making jewellery your principle occupation. Remember to make allowances for unexpected demands on your time: an extra assignment to finish, a sudden domestic crisis, a difficult problem at work.

Be honest in looking at how much time you can use to make jewellery now. You may need to rearrange your life and leave out some interests to give yourself some of that precious extra time. Take some time now to sort yourself out and plan a working schedule. It will save fatigue, disappointment and unrealistic expectations of earning an immediate fortune. (Chapter 4 has details on how to plan your time.)

Space

Jewellery can be made in an amazing variety of places. Some jewellers have used the ironing board, the kitchen table or the bedroom floor as their first work space. Wherever it is, space is needed not only for the actual work but also for the materials and tools. As this is a money-making plan you need enough room for storing materials, somewhere to do your paperwork, space to leave your tools set out as well as an actual workbench. It is partly a time problem. If you have not enough space, you waste time taking out your tools and work and then packing them away again. If there is no room for materials, you waste time buying frequently in small quantities. If you are planning to expand your hobby, more space will be needed. This does not mean you need a huge studio at great expense. It does mean that one of your considerations is space.

Money

Spending money to make money involves a general look at setting up your business. Whether it is now on a large scale or one that will gradually grow, you need to work out your expenses to see if it will be worth the effort.

Materials, tools, stationery, telephone, power, gas, insurance are regular expenses. You will also need some uncommitted money for working capital. It would be foolish to have only enough money to keep one jump ahead. If a shortage of supplies delays delivery dates, you could lose everything — selling contracts as well as your reputation for being a reliable, quality supplier.

Compare your expenses with the money you have available. Will you have enough or will you need to borrow? If you borrow, can you make enough jewellery, as well as sell it, to repay the loan plus interest? Will you earn enough money for the hours you will need to work? This is not meant to be discouraging but it is necessary to look at the money side as well as the creative aspect. Perhaps you may be better off working part-time until you can save enough capital to make a start, meanwhile building your skills and reputation.

Research

I could write much more about the jewellers I know and the problems they found and how they solved them. Some of the research I did is in this book. I recommend you do your own.

Why do other jewellers succeed? Ask them how they started, why they decided to earn their living this way, what problems they found, what advice they can give, and how they are managing. Everyone loves to give advice. Visit workshops and see if you can spend some time with jewellers who can help you answer these questions.

Visit galleries, gift shops, markets and boutiques,

all the places where jewellery is sold. See if there is a market for your type of jewellery and, better still, look for gaps in the market where there is nothing in a certain price range or in the materials with which you work.

Read whatever you can about craftspeople and the problems of going into business. The bibliography at the end of this book will help. There are organizations that can help and advise you too, so do not be shy about using them. Small business agencies in each State, your bank, an accountant, all will advise on various ways to go into business. Some CAE and TAFE colleges have short courses on starting a business. For example, Riverina CAE at Wagga Wagga has a course called *Planning and Starting a New Business.* It consists of a series of cassette tapes and work books. The advice offered by these organizations is not just financial but includes practical and planning advice too.

With all this help and encouragement, plus your talent, enthusiasm, and commonsense you are on your way to a very satisfying career.

Mike Wilson

Mike Wilson is a jeweller who made a spontaneous decision to make jewellery his career and, with hard work, single-mindedness and great enthusiasm, achieved his goals. His biography reads like an adventure novel. Teaching in New Guinea, working as a hospital porter and garage attendant, driving transports and taxis and being a chef are all jobs he has held. During this time he experimented with woodwork, painting, photography and film making, searching for a medium with which he had complete harmony.

As Mike says in the introduction of the catalogue of his tenth exhibition *A decade on...*

'The search came to an end about 1970. I had just finished a year of arts at the University of New South Wales. Wendy, my wife, and I decided to move to Melbourne with our small daughter. Wendy's home was in Melbourne and her brother, Peter, a graduate from the RMIT, School of Gold and Silversmithing had been working with Matcham Skipper. It was these two craftsmen who opened my eyes to what I had been searching for. Within weeks of commencing work with the gold and silver, I had no doubt that this was what I would be doing for the rest of my life. It is now thirteen years later and I am more convinced that ever of this direction.

For three years I spent every spare moment exploring the gold and silver, desperately trying to find a way of becoming completely involved with them. Towards the end of 1973 this finally happened.

I resigned my job as a teacher. Wendy and I sold our family home and with what little equity we had, set up my first workshop in the city of Melbourne. The Crafts Board assisted me with a grant of $600 to obtain some small items of equipment. Wendy returned to her profession as a librarian in order to bring in the steady income that enabled the family to survive. I set up the gallery and workshop to make and market my own designs. I indentured my first apprentice, which then locked me into an 8 to 5 production day, every day. To assist with the enormous development costs I used my own profession as a teacher to run jewellery making classes on three nights per week till 11 p. m. The income and contact with the many and varied students contributed in a multitude of ways to our development and survival in the first three years.'

A positive approach to problems and a supportive partner enabled Mike Wilson to establish himself in a success story that grew out of determination. For most people it would be easier to move gently into a new way of life.

CHAPTER 2

Materials and Tools

Wʜᴀᴛ do you call jewellery? When do you think jewellery is worn? What is its purpose? As a jeweller, have you really thought about these questions? The answers, of course, will differ for everyone. My reason for asking is to encourage you to take the broadest possible view of jewellery, its nature, its function and the materials that can be used to make it.

any time, on any part of the body and have little money value. The reasons for wearing jewellery can be just as varied; as a decoration, to complement clothes, to emphasize the body, to attract attention, to display wealth, for fun, and as a message. Jewellery can take a variety of forms besides the traditional rings, bangles, necklaces and earrings. Traditional jewellery made from precious materials is still the most saleable but jewellery made from inexpensive materials in less conservative form can also sell well.

This chapter is about materials and processes, some of which may be your particular interest, some you may have experimented with and some of which you may never have dreamed. All the materials have been used before with a variety of techniques in pieces which have been sold.

I hope the materials lists will stimulate your imagination and lead you into new areas. I am sure you will find many money-saving ideas for creating jewellery that will sell.

Materials

There are man-made materials and natural materials and all have their own character. Man-made materials have qualities that differ from natural materials. They have a different *feel.* Consider the texture and appearance of the various types of materials and use these differences for contrast and tension in your work. To find this great variety needs just a little lateral thinking and what could be considered as lateral shopping! You will find a guide to craft supplies in the Appendix. But not all supplies come from the specialists. Some come from ordinary places like the hardware store, fishing tackle shop, electronic supermarket, newsagent, chemist, or stationer. Many materials can be found in the garden, on the beach, in the bush, or on the road. Some materials can be recycled from old clothes, old jewellery, obsolete machinery, and kitchen waste. Off cuts and scraps from factories, small components manufactured for other uses and out-of-date samples can all be a cheap supply of unusual materials. The trick is learning not only to look at but to *see* what is around you and to see it in a different context. Exhibit 2-1 lists natural and man-made materials.

Exhibit 2–1   Natural and man-made materials

Natural		Man-made Nonferrous Metals	Ferrous Metals
Amber	Mother of pearl	Gold*	Iron and its alloys
Bamboo	Nuts	Silver*	Steel
Bone	Pearls	Copper	Stainless steel
Coral	Pebbles	Aluminium	
Cork	Pods	Titanium	
Cotton	Seeds	Tantalum	
Egg shell	Shells	Tin and their alloys	
Feathers	Silk	Brass	
Fossils	Skin	Bronze	
Fur	Slate	Nickel silver	
Grass	Soil		
Horn	Stones		
Insects	Teeth	Gilding metal	
Leather	Wood		
Linen	Wool		
Marble			

*Gold and silver are not used in their pure form but as an alloy. Sterling silver, for example, is 925 parts silver and 75 parts copper.

Other kinds of materials are listed in Exhibits 2–2 and 2–3.

Exhibit 2–2   Plastic materials

Thermoplastics	*Thermosetting plastics (casting plastics)*
Acrylic	Epoxy resin
Nylon	Polyester resin
Polyethylene	Acrylic resin
PVC	
Styrene	

Exhibit 2–3   Other materials

Paper	*Miscellaneous*
Cardboard	Ceramics
Cellophane	Glass
Foils	Mirror
Handmade papers	Paint
Photographic paper	Rubber
Tissue paper	
Watercolour paper	

Exhibit 2-4 gives the range of forms in which materials are found.

Exhibit 2–4   The forms in which the materials are available

Metal	Sheet, wire, tube, rod, granules, ingots
Plastic	Liquid, paste, granules, powder, sheet, rod, tube, cloth
Fibre	Hanks, rolls, reels, woven
Leather	Skin, hide, thong, small pieces
Bone	Bones (from the butcher)—boiled and bleached

All these materials have been used many times all over the world, as a glance through a recent jewellery catalogue or a jewellery history book will show. From primitive times, man has decorated himself with a variety of materials.

Our new technology extends the list even further. With the excitement of space research leading to the development of such exotic materials as niobium and the eventual filter-through of new technologies to use by the individual, perhaps the time will come when we wear moon rocks in Jupiter rings!

Processes

Many of the processes used with one material apply to another, particularly metal processes. With ingenuity you can discover new ways of working materials such as using textile techniques for metal or plastics.

Exhibit 2-5   Metal processes

Shape	Saw, file, bend, twist, raise, forge, draw, roll
Heat	Solder, fuse, cast, weld, braze
Join	Rivet, hinge, laminate, bolt, screw, pin, clip
Decorate	Etch, colour by heat, colour with chemicals, inlay, enamel, chase, stamp, engrave, punch, hammer, drill
Finish	Pickle, file, grind, emery, polish, burnish, sandblast.

Electroplating and electroforming are more complicated processes. If you become interested in them, it is possible to take your model to a specialist. There are also many different casting techniques you can experiment with but if you only need to cast occasionally, it is cheaper to make your own wax models and take them to a commercial casting service. If you want to repeat an item, a rubber mould can be made.

Exhibit 2-6   Paper processes

Fold, cut, drill, laminate, sew, mould, tear, roll, crease, pleat, crumple, stretch, twist, emboss, stiffen, colour, dye.

Exhibit 2-7   Fibre processes

Sew, weave, tease, plait, twist, knot, twine, coil, embroider, applique, knit, dye, paint.

Exhibit 2–8   Leather processes

Carve, form, plait, cut, stamp, dye, lace, sew, rivet, laminate, bond.

Work it dry, damp or wet.

When combining leather with metal, the tanning chemicals in the leather may discolour the metal unless the leather is treated with a sealer.

Plastics

Some of the advantages of plastics are their light weight, the wide range of colours, their transparency and opalescence and the way they refract light. Plastics are generally inexpensive, are suitable for mass production and are easily worked with a minimum of tools. Plastics come in two groups:

1   **Thermosetting plastics (casting plastics)** These can be set by heat, pressure or catalyst and then cannot be changed again. The most familiar to jewellers are polyester, acrylic and epoxy resins. These are liquids to which a hardener (catalyst) is added. Resins can be cast in a mould, used as an inlay and to embed other materials, for example, a fragile insect. Another of the thermosetting plastics is a moulding pellet polyester which can be modelled then heatset at a low temperature, for example, polyclay.

2   **Thermo plastics** These can be shaped with heat and changed again with heat. Acetate, acrylic, polyethylene and nylon are all thermo plastics. The most common thermo plastic used by jewellers is acrylic.

Plastics can be used with other plastics and with other materials. Adhesive bonding joins plastics together without changing the surface and solvent bonding softens the surfaces and fuses plastics together. Many of the metal processes can be used with plastic; you can saw, file, bend, twist, hinge, rivet, laminate, drill and polish plastic, Some fibre and paper processes such as pleating, crumpling and embroidering can be used, too. The combination of plastics with different materials and processes is endless.

Tools

You will find a guide to sources of supply in the Appendix.

Metal

A basic list for using with nonferrous metals, which you will want to extend as you progress:

- Four-inch saw frame
- Saw blades 'nought' or 'one'
- Six-inch hand file, No. one cut
- Six-inch ring file, No. one cut
- Six-inch crossing file, No. one cut
- One set of needle files
- One hollow scraper
- Pliers; smooth jawed, round nose, half-round, chain nose, flat jaw.
- Planishing hammer
- Plastic tipped or wooden hammers
- Ring mandrel
- Diagonal wire cutters
- Centre punch
- Scriber

- Steel ruler, square, dividers
- Binding wire
- Soldering tweezers
- Emery cloth
- Polishing compounds
- Hand drill and drill bits

For soldering you will need something to solder on, a gas torch, solder and flux. A soldering pan filled with pumice and set on a lazy Susan bearing is convenient. To solder you will need a comfortable, not too heavy hand-torch which uses gas, either LP, natural, or town. Some jewellers use air as well from either a bellows or a compressor. A glass or plastic bowl for the pickle solution and a tap and sink or bowl of water for washing the pickle from the soldered work are also essential. An extra word of caution here. The pickle solution which is a mixture of acid and water should be handled carefully and any splashes washed off. The granular acid Sparax is less dangerous than sulphuric acid and works just as well. (A book has been written on these health hazards and you will find it listed in the Appendix.)

With these tools you are comfortably set up for making metal jewellery.

As you progress you will want to add to the basic tools and equipment. Hand tools to suit special jobs are probably the next purchase. It is a quite exciting eye opener to go shopping for tools. What you are most likely to choose is a wider variety of files, pliers, hammers and a wider saw frame. It is a very personal selection.

Expenses mount up when you start looking at more sophisticated items of equipment. What you need to decide is if you really need each piece, will it allow you to work more efficiently and faster and therefore be worth the money at this stage in your development. Some pieces of equipment that jewellers acquire after hand tools are:

- A polishing motor with two spindles to use with a variety of buffing wheels and compounds
- An anvil
- A flexible shaft with variable chuck, motor and foot control, burrs, grinders and wheels
- A draw plate and tongs
- A rolling mill
- Riveting, chasing, forging, hammers
- Kiln and casting equipment.

Casting Equipment

This can be a major expense as there are so many pieces involved; kiln, centrifugal casting machine, crucibles, vacuum bell dome and compressor, asbestos gloves, tongs and an oxy acetylene set for greater heat source. There is an alternative and that is to have your wax models professionally cast. Casting can be very useful if you want a lot of one pattern. It allows you to make the piece once and then have as many cast as you need. The rubber mould can be kept for more pieces. The cost can be spread over many pieces instead of just one so it can be a financially rewarding process for production pieces. Casting can also be used creatively for sculptural forms that cannot be easily constructed.

Silversmithing

There are artists for whom silversmithing has a particular appeal but the market for this work is disappearing. It is sheer pleasure to watch an expert raise a bowl effortlessly. There is also a great sense of achievement when you complete your own first small bowl—not without effort—and you realize the years of practice a silversmith needs to work quickly and skilfully. It is not the cost of materials used for silversmithing or the special hammers and stakes needed but the labour cost that handicaps the silversmith who seeks an adequate living.

Forging

Forging is forming the metal by hammering. The metal can be 'moved' to be thinner or thicker depending on where you hammer. When you hammer and compress the metal in one area there will be expansion in another. The jeweller can take advantage of this and create a variation in thicknesses to enhance a design. Size makes no difference, rings, bangles, neckpieces, as well as objects can be forged. Forging can be used in conjunction with other processes to create unusual and interesting pieces. All jewellers need to learn how to forge nonferrous metals accurately and easily as it is a process that has so many uses.

Sharing equipment is an option open to people who live near each other and can work together. An example is sharing a rolling mill or draw bench as you roll a lot of sheet metal at one time or draw down coils of wire and take them to your workshop until you need more. If you are the person with the equipment, you need not be bothered by someone else wanting to use it all the time.

Taking Care of Tools

Tools are an investment and should be looked after carefully. Having a special place to keep them comes first. Even if your tools are in a tool box, that is no excuse for them to knock against each other. Some people make slotted pouches for files, pliers and other small handtools. Hammers can have an old sock on top. Near your work bench you can have a shadow board, a magnetic strip, hooks or a wire to hang a row of pliers over. Mandrels can be kept in holes drilled at the side of the bench and this is where mine are. You will work out a system to suit yourself. (Chapter 3 describes an efficient workshop.)

There are also tools to look after tools! A wire brush for cleaning files is one. If you do not use a tool regularly make sure it is put away clean. Spray with WD40 or oil to inhibit rust or wrap in an oily rag. Hammers can be polished on the buff before using. If you have used your metal tools for other materials like plastics, make sure they are thoroughly clean so one material does not get hammered or caught in another material. Stainless steel and steel will need a separate set of hand tools as the hardness of the metal soon wrecks good tools.

I have thoroughly listed metal tools because these tools can be used for many different materials. Some of the other materials will need special tools and equipment.

1 **Plastics** Accurate scales for the careful weighing of thermosetting plastics, safety equipment such as goggles, dust mask and disposable gloves, and separate buffs and compounds are necessary for working with plastics.

2 **Leather** A properly sharpened knife with a fixed blade for skiving the edge of leather or cutting out, a cutting board, soft lambskin and Dubbin for polishing, special leather dyes and sealer and special needles are all helpful.

I find that I can generally make do or adapt one tool for another use rather than buy a lot more specialist equipment for occasional use. Old files, drill bits, odd shapes of steel, a tyre lever, knitting needles have all been converted into something else.

Learn to use your tools properly, hold them correctly and store them carefully. With care, you will save energy, avoid accidents and not need to replace tools very often.

A jeweller who solved problems of space, tools, and equipment by building, making, and designing his own is Wal van Heeckeren.

Wal van Heeckeren

Wal van Heeckeren arrived in Australia from the United States in September 1968. By January 1969 he had opened the first private School for Silversmiths in Australia at St Leonards, Sydney. Apart from the first three months working for Angus and Coote, Wal has always had his own studio and teaching workshop. An exhibition at David Jones during that first year received wide publicity and helped establish his name.

Part of the publicity was a colour spread of the exhibition in the *Women's Weekly*. 'This publicity was good for five years as people from the country would come in with the article and order from it.' At this time, too, the Argyle Arts Centre opened at The Rocks, Sydney. Wal negotiated a low rental, built his own shop front and as one of the first tenants became a drawcard for other artists. In its early days the Argyle Centre had quite a high reputation as a centre for artists and craftsmen. Wal worked seven days a week often fifteen to eighteen hours a day for seven years while at the Argyle and running his school at St Leonards.

The School for Silversmiths was established as a result of a group of people asking Wal if he would teach. Wal had taught before in the United States and, as he had space in his workshop, the classes were formed. There were three day classes and two evening classes a week with places for eight students. Other days he worked for himself. The tools and equipment for the school were shipped out from Germany and America as most were not available here. 'A little foundry in Edgecliff, H. Plumb, a real family affair, made tinsmith stakes and panel beaters' dollies which was the only pseudo silversmithing equipment I could get.' Wal says, 'At this time, too, individuals were not allowed to hold bullion. You had to be a registered gold user, for example, a dentist or jeweller.'

Wal, who trained at the Rochester Institute of Technology, School for American Craftsmen, has a definite philosophy for his school. The students are exposed to and encouraged to perfect as many techniques as possible, especially in early projects, so they develop such basic skills as planishing, joining metal and making square corners square, etc. 'Eventually projects are left to the students but I make some suggestions to extend their skills.' Wal says, 'I try to encourage students in their own design development, so they are not copies of me, therefore I refuse to get involved in their design decisions. I feel if you have the technique you can make anything work.' He goes on to explain his own approach.

'I've always approached jewellery from the silversmithing point of view because there are so many more silversmithing techniques that apply to jewellery or any kind of metal work. As a result you become a more versatile craftsman and closer to being able to produce, in a three-dimensional world, images that swim round in your head. That is a real skill. I am sad that silversmithing is where it is today and not emphasized in teaching.'

Wal has brought to his teaching more of the American attitudes to craft than the traditional European approach. The American training is different from the European which is more regimented with everyone doing the same exercises. At the Rochester Institute, silversmithing was taught by a Danish silversmith who was not only a superb technician but also willing to look at a student's design no matter how wild. Wal elaborates on this:

'If you really believed in a design and were strong enough in that belief you were allowed to make it. Jewellery was always experimental. Other crafts were in the same building so we were exposed to all crafts. Rochester library also has one of the largest selection of art magazines, books, etc. in America. During the course you did not work as an apprentice but at the end of the four years your final work or masterpiece belonged to the

school. This collection travels and is exhibited all over
the US.'

Wal van Heeckeren's influence on Australian jewellers
was apparent in the 1977 exhibition *Australian Lands-
cape*. Of the twenty-nine exhibitors, one-third had
either worked with Wal (Frank Bauer), for him (Ernst
Pfenninger) or had been his students at some time
(Wendy Manwaring, Barbara Rees, Chris McMaster
among others).

What does Wal think of jewellery today and for the
future in Australia?

'The thirties to forties style still survives but is irrelevant.
On the other hand some of the contemporary work is
exciting idea-wise although sometimes amateurish in
execution. Aside from highly experimental work there
is a mainstream of fashion-conscious buyers who con-
tinue to buy something acceptably different. They will
eventually cause the change of jewellery in the shops
but it will take a number of years. These people do not
want to go too far out.

'The potential buying public for contemporary work
tends to buy whatever is promoted. It does nothing for
the quality of art in Australia or the potential greats
who are growing here. The up-and-coming craftsman
has to work very hard to make it.'

CHAPTER 3

Workshops that Work

WHERE are you going to make these beautiful pieces? How are you going to keep your tools and equipment?

A beginner needs very little space. Your studio does not have to be a large room with elaborate equipment. Your first tools will fit into a tool box and your first workshop can be a strong table. Most jewellers start with creating a space.

Space Search

In the beginning you need a strong table that will not rock, with an edge that will take a clamp and bench pin. After using a table and having to put away your work each time you finish, you will want something more permanent and a jeweller's bench is the next step.

A jeweller's bench can wear many disguises but has certain features in the basic design. The top should be a few inches higher than a standard table height for maximum comfort and it should be thick enough to insert a bench pin. The bench itself must be firm and steady. If you are working with metals, a sliding tray under the bench pin to catch filings and an apron made from soft vinyl or a similar material will catch any other waste. Some side drawers or slots for tools, hooks to hang other tools on or a magnetic strip all help to keep tools tidy and at hand. A jeweller I know used an old roll-top desk. It was a good size, looked like a reasonable piece of furniture when closed and was an attractive solution in a small flat.

My first bench had the necessary features plus a few more. It had a lift-up and fold-back lid and the whole bench pulled out from a laundry cupboard. When I was not using it, I closed the lid and pushed the bench back into place. That kept anything dangerous like sharp tools away from small children. It also gave me a bench top for use in the laundry.

Depending on what materials you use and the type of jewellery you make, a jeweller's bench is all the workshop furniture you may need. Sieglinde Brennan, whose beautiful gum leaf jewellery sells all over Australia, uses a minimum of tools and equipment. She returned to Australia after 14 years overseas and says:

'Working with limited tools, having left most of them in England, forced me to approach my work in a freer and more spontaneous way. I use found, natural materials, gum leaves, bark and shells, copper and brass from a scrap metal merchant, and mass-produced items, fishing wire leads, strings, etc., to create not only wearable jewellery but also visually stimulating pieces which relate to the work process.

'Working with low-cost metals and combining them with either found or mass-produced items stimulates my imagination and enables me to work in a more intuitive way. It also means that the pieces can cost less and are therefore accessible to a wider public.'

Beautiful jewellery, technically perfect, does not necessarily come from a large, well equipped workshop. But you can be frustrated with not having a space to call your own. The laundry is bulging with tools mixed up with clothes or it is impossible to walk around the car in the garage. What next? If you are a budding jeweller living in a flat where you cannot hammer and make a noise, or if there are too many interruptions at home, do not despair. **Access workshops** could be the answer.

An **access workshop** is space that someone else has organized with equipment and spare work benches. Grants to set up this type of workshop have been made by the Crafts Board of the Australia Council. An example of an access workshop is the Messerli Studio in Sydney. The Messerli Studio has space for classes in engraving, jewellery design, jewellery making and stone setting. As well, a few jewellers have their own workbench and space. Torches, polishing machine and anvil are available. Those with their own space pay rent and have access at any time. Their space is not used by the classes.

Shared space is another alternative. Advertise locally for someone with an empty garage or space under their house. Two jewellers I know shared space this way. Taka had rented a basement in a Sydney suburban home which became too expensive for one person so Sylvia Rose shared it. Some of the equipment Taka had was complimented by equipment Sylvia owned, so both benefited. As each had other commitments, it worked out that they only overlapped on two days of the week.

Private teachers who have a workshop classroom

adjacent to their own workshop sometimes come to an arrangement with advanced reliable students to use the students' space on free days. This can be a fortunate arrangement for both as the reliable student has use of the equipment while the teacher is recouping a little money towards the rent.

Community Arts Centres are an option for the jeweller who would like to teach. In return for conducting classes, the jeweller has the use of workshop and equipment.

Shared space, access workshops, community centres, empty classrooms are only a few alternatives to finding a work place away from home.

Do not panic if you are overwhelmed and in a mess at home. Try some lateral thinking. Do you really need a laundry? Put your washing machine and drier in the bathroom and there it is. An ex-laundry workshop with sink, water and power points! Is your garage empty for twelve hours a day while someone drives the car to work? Cars are made from durable materials and can be parked outside twenty-four hours instead of twelve. Build a bench and behold a studio!

Nothing is impossible if you are determined. Is your house on a slope with space underneath? This is how I achieved my workshop. After looking at the space underneath the house, we took a sledge hammer to the carport brick wall, broke through and there were two rooms. Certainly they were full of rock ledges but they had potential. The ceiling was the cement slab of the front entrance, the walls were the brick supports of the stairs; it was ideally fireproof.

The second room had a brick pier in the centre supporting the dining room floor, but the actual space was ten feet by twelve feet. The family and I dug it out to drop the floor to carport level. We hired a jackhammer to break up one large rock, removed the brick pier replacing it with a reinforced steel joist, then poured the floor. The walls were lined and benches built. Shelves and storage eventually followed. The smaller room is my soldering and polishing area, well ventilated and fireproof. Oh yes, I put a window and door in the sledge-hammered hole. Most important, if you are thinking of changes to your house, is to check local building regulations and, if necessary, obtain council permission.

A ready-made garden shed makes a good workshop. One Queensland jeweller included a window wall and an inspiring atmosphere was achieved looking out onto a courtyard garden. Some people, like a Sydney couple whose work compliments each other's, keep digging under their house as they need more room.

So you have either tossed out the washing machine or car, or undermined the house. How do you make the best use of this space? There are four main considerations, the four Ss—size, services, security, safety.

Size

The size of your workshop and your working process will dictate the layout. There is a logical sequence in making jewellery, whatever materials you use, and your workshop plan can help you be efficient.

Plan your own workshop layout by thinking of how you work and observing yourself. Draw it on paper, to scale if necessary, then fit your layout into the space available.

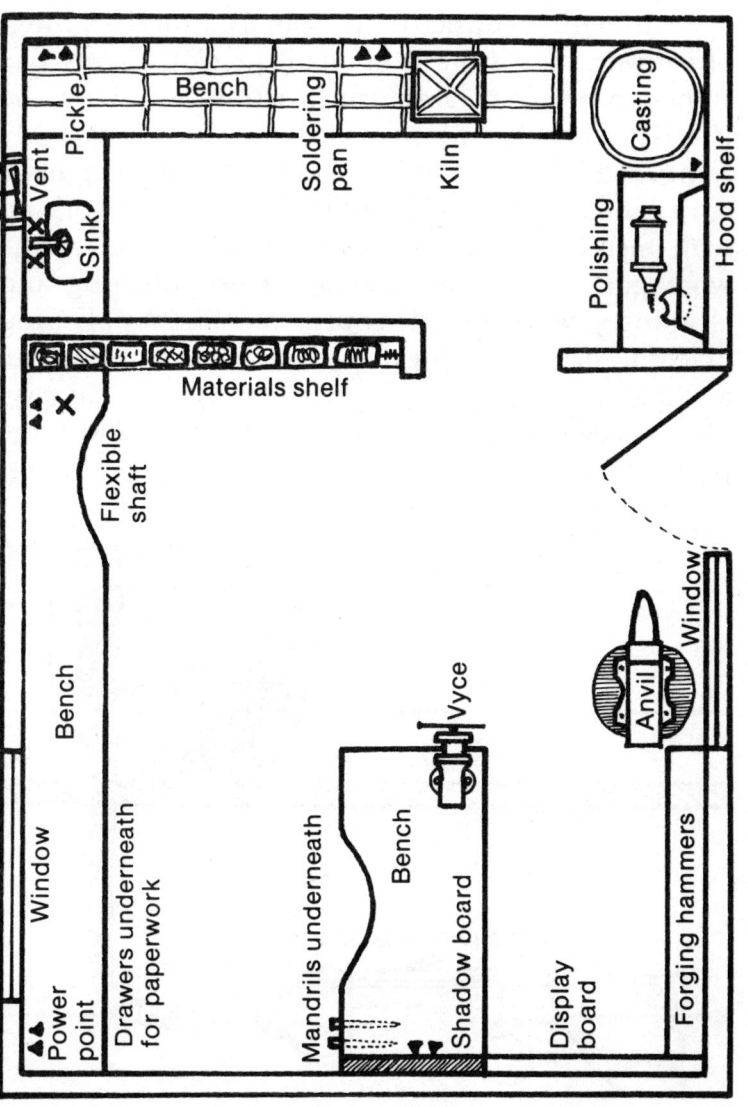

Plan of Workshop

Begin with a cleaner-than-clean area for designing, office work and storage of small precious items like stones. Next, is a clean construction area with the jeweller's bench and space for handtools, probably hung on a shadow board. Drawers, slots and magnetic strip can keep everything at hand. If you are working with metals, the soldering area follows next in the work pattern. The dirty area, where polishing and cleaning of work is carried out, comes last. A polishing machine need not spread dust over everything. Use a shield and some type of extractor system. An easy one is made from an old vacuum cleaner and large plastic bottle.

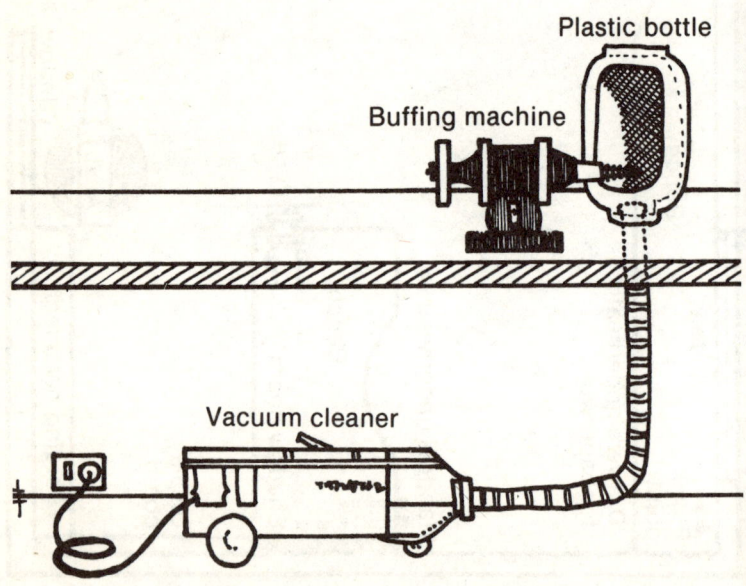

Simple Extractor System

Services

The workshop will need good light, electrical power points, running water and ventilation. Walls with an off-white matte surface help create a soft, non-glare light. Adjustable lamps over special areas will minimize eye strain.

Have twice as many power points as you think you will need. Avoid extension cords and overloading one power point as power tools and equipment soon proliferate. Points will be needed for a flexible shaft, polishing machine, kiln, hotplate and electric jug apart from an extractor fan for fumes. Add a heater in winter and you will see that five double power points would not be too many.

Running water is necessary in your workshop particularly if you are working with acid. Polishing compounds, too, need washing off so a water supply should be available.

Security

Some locked storage and closed cupboards are necessary for acids and other chemicals particularly in a home studio. Finished work needs to be stored carefully and you may wish to have special security for precious metals. Tools and materials need protection from dust and fumes too.

Safety

A checklist for your workshop:

- First-aid kit
- Fire extinguisher, up-to-date
- Heavy equipment bolted down
- Ventilation for fumes from acid, resin, kiln, dust
- Protective clothing for eyes, face, hands.

Other practical considerations are the floor covering, warmth and seating. You may have little choice for the floor. With a cement floor some tools and stones chip when dropped; with boards you can lose small pieces in the cracks. A smooth, light, non-reflective surface would be ideal, such as sheet vinyl, for example.

If you feel the cold, you will need some type of heating as jewellery is mostly a sedentary occupation. I like to forge in winter as it is one way of keeping warm.

So much work is done sitting down that it makes good sense to have the correct chair and bench heights. A chair with an adjustable back for support and castors for moving from one area to the next is useful. Consider room for a comfortable chair for a visitor or those times when you, too, are sitting and thinking.

Some aspects of your studio you may not have thought about will make it a comfortable, pleasant place to work in. Have display boards for oddments that you have collected, design sketches you are considering. Will you have some finished jewellery on show?

Your studio will reflect your personality and your jewellery. Make it a place that is thoughtfully designed and attractive as well as useful, like your jewellery.

Marion Marshall and Daniel Jenkins

Marion Marshall and Daniel Jenkins are partners in Milltons, a jewellery shop and studio in Melbourne. With different training and backgrounds, they have been able to bring to their work a wide range of skills for the making of jewellery as well as in business.

Marion has a diploma in graphic design from the Swinbourne Institute of Technology. As a secondary school art teacher, she first became interested in jewellery when the school where she taught had only metalwork tools in the art department. To be able to teach metalwork, Marion went to part-time classes for further training. Like many people, her first pieces were made at home on the kitchen table. Then deciding that the career she wanted was making jewellery, Marion scraped and saved to finance a two-year goldsmiths' course in Germany.

Daniel, an American, trained at university where he majored in jewellery and then did a two-year trade apprenticeship. University provided a firm background in art history, design, the ability to conceptualize and visualize impressions into forms, and a knowledge of tools and techniques for goldsmithing and silversmithing. The apprenticeship after university enabled Daniel to find a commercial vein through which he could channel his design and technical knowledge as well as provide certain trade skills that would not necessarily apply to art metal students.

Daniel and Marion met in Italy at a summer school with Bruno Martinazzi and they came to Australia early in 1981. To fulfill their dream of being self-employed, they decided to set up their workshop in a craft supply shop in which Marion had a financial interest. They redesigned, revamped and redecorated the shop into a showroom for their own work and a commercial line of fine jewellery that together made an unusual business. The finer, traditional commercial jewellery attracts people wanting a specific adornment or often the client will have something handmade by the partners as an alternative. The bulk of the work is made directly from original design and the making of one-off pieces designed with the client's wishes in mind. Hard work and some compromises have been necessary to survive. Selling 'commercial' jewellery is a compromise of sorts, but it is nevertheless a practical addition to the effort of earning a living as it gives a supplementary money flow. Marion and Daniel believe that their commercial sales help pay for the rudiments of running the business; their one-offs make the business what it is and make Miltons a 'one-off' special kind of shop.

Working together, Marion and Daniel find they support each other when necessary and introduce freshness into each other's discouraged moments. Marion says, 'It stops us stagnating and sometimes we can offer constructive criticism. But being together twenty-four hours a day, seven days a week can lead to unnecessary friction. Another studio at home makes a difference to the work pattern and allows us to experiment and develop new ideas.'

Selling work from their shop has made both partners develop new business skills. When there has been a special advertising campaign, people who come into the shop are asked what brought them in. The window display is constantly changed and this, too, attracts trade. There are two display windows—one always with work of a commercial vein made up of pieces bought from outside sources and some which they make themselves. Some of this work comes from other metal craftspeople and is always of a very high standard. The other window shows the more unusual and larger pieces made by Marion and Daniel, often exhibition pieces which command more attention and may have a special appeal. This double method of display brings the two types of jewellery and other metalwork together and allows a greater variety of clients to be reached as well as show the versatility of the shop.

In the shop, the jewellery is accessible where it can be tried on. Marion can see that more time will have to be spent in the future on marketing. They are both very aware of fashion trends and although they do not set out to keep up with all the changes, they like to be current. Daniel finds selling can be a dilemna for him, not wanting to impose on the public and yet Marion says Daniel is best at handling the difficult people! Marion, on the other hand, is best at the financial side of the business. She says, 'A person's personality has a lot to do with marketing; it's great if you're in control. It's also easier to sell someone else's work and easy to pat someone else on the back!'

Both Daniel and Marion hope to make more of the pieces they enjoy working on now the initial setting up of the studio and shop is complete. 'It is a very valuable experience to have a deadline otherwise you work at the pace the customers set and you do not produce a larger range.' Marion is planning more one-off pieces in steel and gold while Daniel, as well as continuing his hollow-formed heat-coloured copper pieces, is producing a range of bronze bells with varying tonal qualities and colours. The bells should sell well as they have a very Australian look about them. Something which is popular or special with clients is the use of repoussé in so much of the work. Repoussé is such a distinctive technique that people who are after a special look, know that a hollow or special form can be requested. Casting is rarely used because of Daniel and Marion's ability to shape metal and create a great variety of surface details with handtools. Specializing is important for the business and their customers know that the shop will cater to the individual.

CHAPTER 4

Getting It All Together

Iᴛ is vital to plan your time to make the best use of it, to keep out of a mess and avoid expensive mistakes. A successful business needs planning in every area: time to experiment, time to make individual pieces and to develop production or multiple pieces. Production work, the basis of a successful business, needs careful planning in all its processes. You will want to balance the number of multiple pieces which sell easily with the individual pieces which may take more time and not sell quite so well. So learn to plan your time as carefully as you plan a new piece of jewellery.

If you don't know where to start or how to sort yourself out to plan your time, it's helpful to write down everything you do and how long it takes. Keep a track record of how you use your time for several weeks or longer, if necessary. You'll be surprised how much time you have and what scant use you make of it. From this survey you will see that where you are spending time comes under headings such as making, buying, cleaning and thinking, to name just a few. Under these headings, list every aspect of work connected with that activity and how long it takes. Include how often you need to do that task.

Buying materials is an example. You might check supplies in the workshop, 15 minutes; telephone suppliers to see if what you need is available, thirty minutes; drive to the city, park, walk to shop, one hour; buy products, thirty minutes; return home, one hour; put away materials, fifteen minutes. So buying supplies has actually taken three and a half hours. How often are supplies bought? Perhaps once a month. So in your time survey you would put down three and a half hours once a month to buy supplies. Some things will happen weekly, monthly, or even yearly. It is important to include everthing because any task left out will need to be sandwiched in at some time and this produces pressure.

From this survey, draw up a simple timetable. It need not be rigidly adhered to but it will help you make spaces for all the things you need to do and help you to be flexible enough to cope with any emergencies. In the beginning, a timetable will help you set a reasonable delivery date for orders. With a system that allows spaces for checking materials before starting a project and time for something unexpected happening, you will be able to work with full concentration and no hassles.

The things to think through thoroughly and include in your timetable are:

- Ideas
- Experimenting
- Planning a piece
- Test pieces
- Making the jewellery

- Buying materials
- Photographing work
- Paper work, bookkeeping
- Selling
- Market research
- Review of work
- Cleaning workshop
- Relaxation

The Design

The planning of a new work from the idea, through experimenting, to a test piece, and finally making the piece is all *design*.

One of the most pleasant parts of making jewellery and one that needs plenty of time is planning and creating a new piece. A brilliant inspiration may be a blinding flash in the mind, but that idea needs a lot of work before it's translated into a satisfying piece of jewellery. Have you worked your idea right through to its very essence? Can it be extended in other ways? The first sketches will work out the basic line, shape and size. Do the sketches need more work to make them finished drawings to show clients or retailers? Are the drawings to be part of an exhibition? Having worked out the basic sketches, all the other decisions have to be made; what materials to use, whether or not it can be a production piece and where it will fit into the market.

Thinking through every aspect of a new piece at this early stage will save expensive mistakes later. At this point some jewellers make models from other materials such as paper, cardboard, or aluminium, pinned, glued, or stapled together. Plasticine is also useful for models. These pieces can be used as a pattern after all the adjustments have been made. The next step may be to make a test piece. When you make a test piece you will know how much the materials will cost and have some idea of the labour involved. What if the cost is too high? Can the materials be changed to less expensive ones? Go back to the drawing board to simplify the idea so that labour will take less time.

Having solved these problems, have you a piece that is suitable for multiple production? If the piece can be produced efficiently in quantity at a price and in a style that has sales acceptance, the answer is yes. Remember to include the experimental time in your costing. If you have made several test pieces before finding a satisfactory production design, these pieces can still be sold as a series.

It is also worth thinking that some components of a production piece may be used in other pieces. An obvious example is a series of links that can be used for a short necklet, a long chain, or a bracelet. When making units for a chain, make more than are necessary for one chain; make enough for three or four pieces at the one time. There are two advantages as avoiding repetition of the one process will save time and be more efficient. You will also become so practised and skilful that not only will you work efficiently and smoothly, but you will find you can concentrate more on refining the piece. Remember that time taken to produce so many components will be spread over more than one piece of work.

Buying Materials

A well organized workshop where you can see your materials and know what you have saves time and patience. We have all said at one time or another after searching through stacks of precious junk, 'I know I have one somewhere but I just cannot find it.' Keeping your materials neatly stored will not only save time but will prevent damage or breakage. Scratched metal that has not been put away carefully costs money in work and time. Not all materials and tools are readily available in all States. Some need to be chased and tracked down. If you live near the city use the telephone. Instead of buying one item at a time, check the suppliers by telephone to see that what you need is in stock and then make one trip for everything on your list.

If you live in the country you will need to keep a closer watch on your materials. Keep in stock as much as you can possibly afford. When writing for supplies, allow time for the vagaries of the Post Office. Remember to include any postage charges or delivery costs in your overhead costs.

Allow time when shopping to look at new products, visit a new supplier or just browse to see what is new or different.

Bulk buying can be an advantage. Some things like findings, for example, are cheaper if bought in quantity. The price of sterling silver earring hooks with safety catch changes considerably from $1.40 for one pair to $90 for one hundred pairs, including sales tax which means a saving of $50. Some materials such as some types of stainless steel are only available in large amounts. See if you can find another jeweller or group of jewellers who can share in bulk buying to make it worthwhile.

There are also *disadvantages* to bulk buying and you will need to balance the advantages against the disadvantages. Capital can be tied up for a long time if you are not using a lot of the material or using it very often. Some products have a limited shelf life. Resins, for example can be expensive and deteriorate quickly, and yet are not always available in small quantities. These disadvantages can be another reason to find other jewellers or craftspeople to share in bulk buying.

Labelling your materials with the date purchased, shelf life and price paid can be a timesaver. A glance at a label on a can of resin will tell you quickly how much longer you can use it.

Keeping up-to-date records of the cost of material and the quantity you have is a necessary part of pricing and financial management (See Chapter 7).

Records

Taking a photograph of your work when it is finished should become a habit. Keep a record of your pieces for several reasons: your portfolio, insurance, publicity, and to show clients. If you have a good camera and know how to use it you can take the photographs yourself, or alternatively ask a photographer friend to help. Be aware that photographing jewellery can be very difficult because of the small size of the work and reflections from polished surfaces. If you are not competent with a camera, you can have your work professionally photographed. This may end up cheaper and worthwhile in the long run. When you want a clear photograph for a newspaper or your own publicity, you will need a good black and white print. If you are submitting slides for exhibition selection or to an interstate specialist shop you will also need an expert job. At times like this it will certainly pay to have your work professionally photographed. This becomes one of your business expenses.

Paperwork

As with any business there is always the paperwork. Keeping records of materials, what is made, where your work is, and if it's on consignment, what money you are spending, and what money is coming in will all take time. All these aspects of fighting the paper war are in Chapter 7. The reason they are listed here is because it can take an incredible amount of time, particularly in the beginning, to keep your records. If you are going to be super efficient in your timetable, set aside some time each day to write up your records. If you become accustomed to doing so on a daily basis and then at the end of the week, totalling hours, expenses, materials used, etc., you will find it much easier to balance your books each month. It sounds like a lot of time but it need not be and the more you do book work the faster you will become.

Selling

The techniques of selling and promotion are discussed in Chapter 6 but it is wise to set aside time each month to contact all your existing outlets or to look for new ones. You will need time to call or make appointments with both old and new clients. Once you have become established it may not be necessary to ring first, but in the beginning, set aside time for telephoning as well as visiting your customers.

Are you going to have an open studio every few months, or organized group visits? Remember to plan time for getting your studio ready, checking work to see that it is priced, checking cards or any other promotional material to see that everything is available. Remember that there is no profit in your work until it's sold, so give yourself adequate time for this important aspect of your business.

Market Research

Casing the market is something that can be partly done while you are doing other things such as shopping. While you are out buying supplies you can browse through some of the stores to see what is being sold. Check on what the commerical jewellers have, at what prices, and to see what is fashionable. Research can also be done when you are selling your work whether it is through talking to someone in your workshop or when you deliver your work to a specialist shop. It is worthwhile every now and then to decide that you are going to take time out to look at what is happening in the market-place. It may be to look at next season's fashions or it may be time to visit a street market you have not been to before. Whatever form your market research takes, remember to make allowances for it in your timetable.

Review Of Work

As a result of your market research, or after an exhibition or completing a production run, you will want to review your work. This is important for your survival and therefore needs a decent slot of time in your timetable. Put it in the morning when you are fresh and thinking clearly. A few hours in the morning should be enough time if it is something you do regularly.

Basically, it's sitting down with pen and paper and making a list of everything that was right and anything that was wrong. This can apply to pieces of work right through to a whole exhibition or to a sales promotion. Write down what you would do differently while it is still fresh in your mind. If any new ideas come through, write them down before you forget.

When you are reviewing your work, some considerations will take you right back to the original concept. Did the piece of jewellery work out as planned? Were you able to make as many pieces from the materials as you estimated? Once the pieces were made in quantity, did the time, labour, and materials work out as expected? For a fast-selling design, write down what the selling points were and any feedback you have had. When reviewing a group of pieces, try to find out which sold first and why, as well as why the others did not sell. It is more then merely interesting to analyse your sales; it is necessary so you can compare the actual results with the reasons you decided to make these prices. So include reviewing work as a regular part of you timetable.

Quality Control

When you are making a lot of the same design, how will you know that piece number five is the same as piece number twenty-two? Will you be able to guarantee that the twenty pieces ordered by a shop are the same as the ten they have just sold? Making sure that the pieces are the same is part of quality control and one of the things you must learn to watch carefully and allow for in your timing. The test pieces you made when working out your production piece may be your prototypes for quality control. What is needed is one piece which all the other pieces of the design can be compared with. When you have made the first series, look at them carefully to check that everything is as it should be: the parts work, the finish is perfect and all pieces are similar. Take one that is typical of the group and keep it. When you are making another run of that series, you then have an original for comparison.

That is one aspect of quality control that applies to multiples and should only need half an hour when checking finished work. The other kind of quality control is exactly that—quality. Do not allow any piece of work to leave your workshop if you are not happy with it. It is sure to boomerang back in an uncomfortable way. Every piece should be as technically perfect as you can make it. This will take time, not only in checking the finished work, but every step of the way.

This is different from jewellers saying, 'I would really like to do something more with this piece'. That is not querying the quality! It is their creativity spurring them on!

Clean Up

Do you, like many craftspeople, work in a controlled mess? Sometimes a mess can threaten to swamp you completely. If so, it's time for a clean up. After you have worked through and finished one series is a good time to clean up and move on to something new. It can put a full stop to the finished idea and remove any distractions. Mess does niggle at one's conscience.

At the end of a production run, add an hour or two on your timetable to clear away materials from that job and generally tidy the workshop. It is a particularly good idea to clean your workshop if the materials from the previous job are different and incompatible with the new work. Enamelling is a good example as it needs particularly clean areas.

If you have a yearly blitz, use a vacuum cleaner—a household one with paper bag liner or hire an industrial cleaner. For jewellers who are working with precious metals the amount of precious dust sucked up can be worth taking to the refiners. Depending on how tidy you have been throughout the year, your workshop may only need half a day to thoroughly sort out old materials and clean all spaces and equipment.

Relaxation

Walk on the beach, walk through the bush, have a day in the city. Whatever you enjoy, take a day off to do it. Of course creating beautiful jewellery and making it need not be considered hard work if you really enjoy what you are doing. However, you need to be fresh and not subject to eye strain. We are not computers plugged in to work twenty-four hours a day. Work that is repetitive, done constantly, can be tiring; we get careless, make mistakes, then waste a piece. Time spent relaxing is not time wasted. Often it will be the time for new inspiration, that blinding flash, which brings us back to the beginning of the cycle—design.

These are the factors you need to look at when drawing up your timetable, and you may find a few of your own to add. If it seems an overwhelming number of things to do and keep track of, just think of the job you are doing now. In your present job you probably plan and allocate your time to suit other staff, travelling time and somewhere to fit in your personal life. With your own jewellery-making business you will have a great deal of flexibility. In your own timetable, you can take into account whether you are an early bird or a night owl and what time of day you work best and most productively. You can timetable for children, outings or hot summer weather. You can plan the routine tasks to be broken up by the most interesting ones. You can also plan to work hard for seven days or more in a row and not take a conventional weekend.

Whenever I have something new to do or a busy schedule, I plan it on paper. This book and the time to write it had a plan: so much a week, time for research, time to think and spare time in case of troubles. As writing is a new occupation for me, I tried to work each chapter into a schedule. I will use my plan and timetable shown opposite as examples of how I considered every detail.

The weekly timetable included extra time for exercise as I thought sitting and writing for so many hours

Exhibit 4–1 Plan for book

Time allowed	Six months
February	Two chapters as expect to be slow in beginning
March	Three chapters
April	Three chapters
May	Interviews with jewellers visiting Sydney for Expo
June	Writing interviews and slotting in to the whole
July	Corrections, and then copy typed
August	Index, could not be done until copy typed.

Extra load during these months had to be allowed for; school holidays in May, technical college assessments in July, unexpected virus in July.

Exhibit 4–2 Weekly Timetable

	Monday	*Tuesday*	*Wednesday*	*Thursday/Friday*
8 a.m.	Swim	Swim	Swim	Technical college both days
9 a.m.	Housework	Housework	Housework	
10 a.m.	Write	Write	Research	
3 p.m.	Lunch, exercise, relax telephone			
4 p.m.	Write	Write	Interviews	
6 p.m.	Put away all papers, etc. shopping			

a day needed the balance of more than usual time for swimming and running. In the morning, while fresh, I would do the first drafts. In the afternoon, I rewrote and tidied the morning's effort. As I did not have a permanent desk, time had to be allowed to put away papers, pens and reference books which was a continual nuisance. Wednesdays were used for research, talking to other jewellers, telephoning and writing letters as well as fitting in household shopping. Many aspects of writing a book were not included in the original timetable and I had to make some adjustments. I found I needed more time to read reference books, for example. Another was fitting in with other people's availability. Where I might have allowed a week or two between the first and second contact, it often ran into four or five.

Be prepared to make adjustments to your timetable and you will soon find you are benefiting from a more efficient work pattern.

Dorothy Erickson

A jeweller who worked to a long-range plan to achieve what she wanted is Dorothy Erickson.

Dorothy Erickson is a jeweller from Perth with an Australia-wide reputation. While studying for an arts degree she decided to specialize in jewellery but at that time there were only elective jewellery courses in Western Australia. She learned by going to trade experts in various fields and so built up a range of techniques—casting learned from a dentist; stone setting from a Greek; box making—forging and raising from other jewellers. Other techniques were self-taught from books. Later she majored in jewellery as part of a design degree.

Long-range planning has been the basis of Dorothy's success. She decided to teach until her home workshop was fully equipped and paid for. During this time she lectured at the Western Australia Institute of Technology and used the college workshop. Dorothy continued to teach until she had enough money to live on for a year, buy materials and have working capital.

Another decision she made was not to sell anything until her first solo exhibition so she could, in her own words, 'come in with impact'. For this exhibition Dorothy designed the invitations, arranged press releases and set up the exhibition. She decided the walls were too bare, so covered them with photographs. She used all the possible selling tricks. As the exhibition was an outstanding success, all the detailed planning paid off. Dorothy's philosophy is, 'I won't approach anything until I can do it properly'. The variety in her work and the markets covered by Dorothy Erickson are the result of market research. There is a production range, a designer range and a limited edition series. Before Christmas she makes a group of 'pretties', better described as a gift line. Her work is available at specialist shops in every capital city. As well, she has a gallery exhibition once a year.

To be successful it has been necessary for Dorothy to compromise, not in workmanship or quality, but by continuing to make pieces from a successful series when requested, although that series may be finished. Not to mass-produce is another compromise. As Dorothy says, 'I will compromise to enable myself to survive but not to ruin my future'.

With plans for an exhibition in Europe and a continuing slice of the Australian market, Dorothy Erickson is an example of a purposeful jeweller who knew what she wanted and planned how to achieve it.

CHAPTER 5

Projecting Your Image

THE way you present yourself as a jeweller in a competitive market-place needs a well planned approach for immediate impact. In planning the promotion of your work and your image as a craftsperson, all aspects of presentation will need to be considered. You are designing a public picture of yourself and your work which is easily recognizable, well organized, and immediately states your professionalism. Each part of your presentation must be designed to function efficiently as a unit as well as reinforcing the whole image. This will include your jewellery stamp, labelling and packaging, letterhead and business stationery, business card, price lists, catalogues or brochures, and your portfolio. Personal appearance is important, too. Jewellers need to wear their work.

The Jewellery Stamp

Your jewellery stamp is a good starting point for your presentation. The stamp is how you sign your work so it is necessarily small but still needs to be easily read. Whatever you are making—metal, plastic, or leather jewellery, or using a variety of materials—it should be possible to sign your work. Some jewellers use their initials, others a symbol, some use both; others like to put a row of stamps with their initial, year, type of metal, Australia and 'handmade'. The pattern or variety of these stamps becomes part of that jeweller's identification and image.

Labelling and Letterhead

Any business uses a range of paper in various forms. You will need invoices, a letterhead, labels and business cards and most of them will require your name, address, phone number and occupation. You can also include your jewellery stamp as a logo. A rubber stamp could be useful and less expensive in the beginning as an alternative to commercial printing. Stationers and specialist office suppliers can make up a simple stamp for you. Special designs, such as your jewellery stamp, can be produced as a rubber stamp if a simple black and white drawing of the correct size is supplied. As this is to be cut out, avoid fine lines which cannot be successfully produced in rubber. From the time you start contacting people you need business cards, and probably letterhead paper. These are not expensive and are a good way to leave your name and address with prospective customers and when using the mail. A sense of professionalism is shown by coordinating business stationery which uses one style of lettering, paper and ink colour. Although labels to tie on your jewellery can be small white swing tags from the news-agent, something more personal will reinforce your other items. If the materials used in a particular piece of jewellery need special care or cleaning you can write it on a larger label. Label and price your jewellery as you finish each piece so if someone calls at your workshop, the price is readily available.

Exhibitions

When you have an exhibition or sale, maintain any theme or new direction in your work in the design of the invitations, advertising and leaflets. Try to be different. For a few years every craftsperson seemed to use earthy tones in ink and roughly textured paper and it all became predictable and lifeless. What a contrast it was to receive an invitation on a crisp, white card with bold red print! Avoid being the same as everyone else—your individuality is important. Plan to have each printed item visually reinforce the others and once you're established, remember that variations and changes can be considered.

Packaging

Think carefully how you will package your jewellery to protect it and to present it effectively. Jewellery is often purchased as a gift so the package can also act as a form of giftwrapping. It can also provide a neat way of storing a piece for the buyer. Some jewellers use boxes, some make velvet, suede or cotton bags. Paper, too, can be folded into attractive envelopes or little bags and used for gift packages. Some chain stores sell tiny odd shaped baskets and other containers which are cheap and unusual. Jewellery suppliers have the more conventional velvet and plastic cases. One jeweller I know made soft plastic bubbles so that the piece inside looked most attractive and unusual as well as being well protected. Whatever you choose, include your stamp design or name on the outside of the package so it will be easily identifiable.

Self-Promotion

Wearing your own jewellery is one of the best ways to reinforce your image. I am astounded by the number of jewellers who wear no jewellery at all. I have even been to an exhibition of a group of jewellers where not one of them wore a piece of their own work at the opening. Were they saying our pieces are great in a display case but unwearable? Every jeweller must have a few pieces of work that say this is me, this is my style. I took self-promotion a step further by making a bulky jumper with six of my recent jewellery designs plus my stamp knitted into the pattern. Friends recognized the designs and other people stopped me to ask about it. So, besides being fun to make, and looking attractive, and keeping me warm, it was also a boost for my jewellery.

Portfolio

A portfolio is a portable information file. It is used to sell yourself to shops who may buy your work, or for gallery directors planning exhibitions and in any new situation where you want to introduce yourself. A portfolio will say who you are, what you can do and what you have done. As well as photographs of your work, a portfolio can include actual samples if the pieces are small and easy to carry. As jewellers we are fortunate, as our work is easily displayed. A portfolio should be comprehensive and cover most aspects of a jeweller's work, but should not be so extensive that it overwhelms the viewer.

Let's suppose you have an appointment for an interview. If you have not used your portfolio for some time you will need to check through the information to make sure it is up-to-date. It should also be possible to rearrange the information to suit the interview you are having. For instance a gallery director would want to see examples of your individual exhibition pieces, the quality of your work, the range of materials and techniques used. Some gallery directors like to see how ideas and work develop so photographs showing some processes may be useful. Galleries need to survive, too, so if it is an interview for a selling exhibition, they will be calculating which pieces will suit their clients. If you have an appointment with a retail shop you will need different information. The range of designs, size and prices of work, the quantity you can supply, how it is packaged, and when you can deliver will be listed information you can show with the samples. (See Chapter 6 for pointers on interviews.)

Your portfolio can be quite simple when you are a beginner as you may not have much information to list. Nevertheless, everyone has a statement to make. You can list who you are, what you are doing, why you are doing it, where and how. Avoid being carried away but try to include a little of your philosophy. Later you can include experience, exhibitions, special awards and collections where your work is included. Some people include a personal photograph. Whatever you put in your biography, it should be easily read and relevant. Some retailers like to tell their customers about the artists and how they work as it helps to sell the piece.

Photographs and drawings of work will be included in your portfolio. If there is a particularly interesting detail, you can draw attention to it with an elaborated drawing or close-up photograph. Make sure an indication of the size of the piece is included. To keep photographs and drawings flat, clean and easily handled and enable changes to be made, a ring binder file is useful. Ring binders come in many sizes, and stationers and art suppliers have a wide selection so choose one to suit the size of photograph and drawing, and check that the size is readily available. When putting photographs and drawings in the plastic pockets make sure they all face the same way so the folder does not have to be turned around continually.

Carrying pieces of jewellery to show clients takes some thought and preparation, too, as you need a system to keep the jewellery protected and still be easy to unpack and display. Traditional or valuable jewellery can be carried in velvet or suede lined cases, either in individual containers or larger ones with compartments for each piece. Alternative-material pieces can be displayed with more imagination. Leather jewellery can be carried in matching skin bags, and wood, shell, and feather jewellery in a natural cane basket.

Quite a few jewellers plan a container or means of displaying their work at the same time as they design the jewellery. Wendy Manwaring mounts some of her pendants in wood with special grooves for the chain. While this is more appropriate for galleries there is no reason why similar, less complicated systems cannot be devised for showing work to retailers. If you do not want to make a case to carry your work, search for a ready-made container that would be appropriate in size and style. Antique boxes, small leather chests, make-up cases, zip-open handbags, art deco velvet bags and artists' folders can all be used.

Your portfolio now consists of your biography, photographs, drawings, samples and perhaps a catalogue or brochure. All this information can be collated in various ways. You can arrange it chronologically with the most recent work appearing first, then working backwards, or thematically if you have been working this way, or by grouping it by techniques or materials. An example of this arrangement would be to have photographs of all enamel work together, then all pieces with stone settings. Another way would be to put all the photographs of neckpieces together, then rings, objects and so on. These arrangements can be varied to suit each individual interview.

Captions will be needed for photographs and drawings stating size, materials, techniques, and price. Explanations may be needed with some pieces, not just 'silver neckpiece with coral', for example, but 'hinged sterling silver neckpiece incorporating coral worm found by client at Barrier Reef'. This is a more interesting caption that also subtly says you undertake commissions, use unusual materials, and can make a technically difficult hinge. For all your captions, be consistent in the use of capitals and small letters, underlines and headings. Choose from handwriting, typewriting, stencil or transfer lettering. The layout of a page is important, too. Use uniform sizes of photographs and margins, and uniform ways of placing captions and headings, as well as consistent spacing. Once you have a system, maintain it, as this will make your task easier as well as look more professional.

Publicity

Having established your image as a professional craft jeweller you can now promote and publicize it. Most publicity is free while advertising is paid for, so, naturally, what we are looking for is publicity. As a beginner, the easiest way to start is by establishing yourself locally. Newspapers and radio are the usual places to try apart from contacting local groups and doing some personal promotion. Chapter 6 discusses how to make use of local organizations and where to find them as well as other ways of personally promoting your work.

Newspapers

Most suburbs and small towns have local newspapers so this is an option available to everyone. But because local newspapers are so available and depend on local interest stories, there is keen competition to place an article. The way to get your story featured is simple if you follow the rules.

Your press release should be short and to the point. It needs to be typed with double spacing without spelling mistakes or any other corrections. At the top of the page put a catchy heading; at the foot your name, address, and telephone number. If you are including a photograph, a clear black and white print is acceptable. The main features of your press release should be an opening 'grabber' for the first sentence and an original angle on the information. Unless you immediately catch the reader's interest and have a different angle, no matter how well written your story, it would not be printed. As an example, I used this approach for an article in the local paper which has a reputation for being choosy about its articles. I had read a short piece about two people selling Christmas cards that played a carol. I cut the article and its photo from the paper and clipped it to my letter which read:

Not only musical Christmas Cards! What about electronic jewellery that plays four carols and has twinkling lights as well? Electronic jewellery made by Robin Stubbs will be exhibited next week at the Christmas Show at—

Then followed brief details. At the end I put 'for more information please ring' and gave my phone number. The result was a call from the paper who sent out a photographer/reporter. Later in the week there was a great article and photograph which helped publicize the Christmas Show. The attention grabber was the electronic jewellery and tying the information to the previous article. The approach worked because I had something new to say and a different way of saying it. I also sent the letter out clearly and hand-delivered it so it arrived promptly after the first article. I then made sure I would be at home if the paper were to telephone during the next few days.

Most newspapers have a diary column or a supplement once a week which lists local events in the arts and entertainment scenes. Diary columns or supplements rely on information given to them and if it is clearly written and concise, it is sure to be printed. If you are supplying information to several papers, vary the content so each paper has something individual. An interesting item may even lead to a feature story, so write that opening sentence carefully.

When you are successful in having an article printed in the paper, cut it out, with the date and the newspaper masthead, then photocopy all three. Use the photocopies to show clients, post to local groups looking for guest speakers, or use on shop notice boards when publicizing a show, or even at the local library when part of a local crafts group. There are many ways you can recycle the original article for extra mileage.

Do you live in an attractive area where the local tourist association organizes publicity? Many tourist committees publish brochures on what to see in their area and you may be able to have your studio and work written up as worthy of a visit. For example, the historic town of Braidwood, New South Wales, has a tourist brochure which includes an article about Christoph Altenburg's sterling silver jewellery and his craft shop in the old Bank of New South Wales.

Radio

It is harder to find ways of publicizing your work through the radio although opportunities do exist. Some stations have a weekly segment with items of public interest, charity activities, and interviews in the programme. The same way of supplying information to radio stations applies as it does to newspapers. Be clear, concise, capture interest with your opening. A few towns and suburbs have access radio stations which specialize in local news and events so these are worth finding. It is a matter of knowing your local scene and using it.

Displays

Some public buildings feature displays of work or publicity material of local interest. I have seen promotions by arts and crafts groups, charities and sporting organizations in a variety of places including shopping centres, libraries, council chambers, banks, hotel foyers and clubs. Some of these places have a manager or promotions secretary who can be contacted personally. At other places try to find who is in charge and make appointments. You can then offer whatever you think is most appropriate for the location. Have your material worked out before an appointment and then present it the same way you would at any interview.

Wherever you try to place publicity material, remember that you are requesting something for nothing and it is quite likely you will have no control over how it is displayed. If you are successful, do follow up with a 'thank you' letter paving the way for your welcome another time.

When you have found a number of places that will help you with publicity, make a list of them and keep adding to that list as you find more. You will build a useful file of names, addresses and telephone numbers. Keep a record of when you contact them and when you are successful, so as not to overload one helpful source too often.

You now have a package on how to present yourself as a jeweller in a competitive market. It can be used to explain or elaborate on what you say or it can stand alone as your representative. Use part of it, build on it gradually or establish a complete system, depending on your needs. Look ahead and be flexible enough to change and add units in the future. If well organized now, your presentation should be simple to maintain and work efficiently for you.

Presentations

Every jeweller has different ways of presenting individual and exhibition pieces from the multiple series and production items shown in the catalogue, brochure and print out sheet. Following are some examples.

Dorothy Erickson has carefully worked out her presentation. It consists of a four-page brochure with coloured and black and white reproductions of her multiple series jewellery. Inside the front cover is her biography. Then follows a detailed description of each piece, a suggested retail price list and terms, and a list of selected retailers where her jewellery is available.

A different approach is used by Mike Wilson. His catalogue is a card folder with an inside pocket. The folder has Mike's biography and photograph plus a list of his retailers. This is information which remains constant. The pocket has five loose pages of black and white reproductions of his production jewellery as well as a one-page price list and a page with mail order forms and mailing list. The pocket system allows changes to be made by deleting or increasing the number of pages and changing the price list when necessary.

A computer print out sheet is used by Lyn Tune for her individual fashion range. This sheet, shows the design, colour range, price and order number. Agents can use it for orders, or it can be left with outlets for reorders. It works well, is a fast information source for Lyn and is a novel way of presenting vital information.

CHAPTER 6

Selling and Surviving

In Chapter 1 you assessed your skills and motivation as a jeweller and decided that you would try to support yourself by your craft. Now five chapters and some time later you are probably anxious about selling it. Take heart! Just as you have learned to make jewellery, you can also learn to sell it.

Be realistic. Your aim is to sell and make extra money. Have the confidence to know your work is good and of course it will sell. Be aware of the standard of workmanship and artistic values and do not compromise in these areas. If your work is good, people *will* buy.

The satisfaction of selling comes from working through the whole process from the initial idea, through making to finally seeing someone choose your work and wear it with pleasure. Few occupations offer such complete involvement and satisfaction. Selling needs planning. We all start by selling from our workshops but look ahead and consider all the options; workshop, community contacts, local shops, specialist shops, markets, and galleries.

Workshop Sales

It is flattering when you are a beginner to have people come to you for your work. You are in control of the process from the development of an idea through the making to the actual wearing. Talking to clients can be a source of ideas and stimulation. It is one way to move easily into selling as you can learn not only to be businesslike about your pieces but to discuss their featured points as well.

Most beginning jewellers, through modesty and inexperience, ask too low a price at first. For the same reasons customers will often offer less than a realistic price and with friends it becomes even more difficult to discuss money. You will learn the first lesson when you discover that you are selling your work at a price that allows nothing for your labour. If you value your work, others will, too.

If you are embarrassed about discussing money, then label your pieces with the price or have a current price list available. Everyone is accustomed to price tags for professional wares. Whatever you do, avoid working out a price on the spot.

When selling from the workshop, look ahead—your time is money. You cannot afford to be sidetracked by too many casual callers. If this is happening, send out a pleasant letter to customers saying that you will be happy to see them by appointment and that your studio is open at certain hours on nominated days. Extend this system to having an open workshop or studio exhibition of your work every six or twelve months. Many artists do this particularly before Christmas.

For ten years I had a studio exhibition on the first weekend in November. When I started there was one other craftsperson, a potter doing the same thing in my local area. The first year I invited about sixty people. Ten years later, I had a guest list of three hundred and fifty. During that time I learned so much, made many friends and enjoyed myself, as well. Details are at the end of this chapter under 'Workshop Exhibitions'.

Community Contacts

One of the ways to become known and sell your work is through contact with people in your area. Very few people know how jewellery is made and are eager to listen when you start explaining the process to them. Become a guest speaker or a demonstrator. There are many community groups looking for guest speakers at their meetings. School groups, service clubs, special interest groups are all worth contacting. Look in your local newspaper to see what activities these groups are organizing. The local council often has a handbook listing community organizations. Write to the groups saying what you can do and offer your services. You can offer a variety of services such as a demonstration, a talk, a small display or an open day at your workshop for a limited number. It could be offered as a form of fund raising for that group.

Just north of Sydney there used to be a little gallery shop called the Catalyst. It was only a garage and shed with some grass outside but it spilled over with crafts and enthusiastic buyers. One of the main reasons was that the owners held regular coffee mornings or afternoons when a group would visit by arrangement. One of the craftspeople would talk, demonstrate, or discuss, and generally promote their own work. The visiting group received 5 per cent of all sales, the owners sold well to a captive audience and took 20 per cent commission and the visiting craftsperson did extremely well. A very clever way of selling.

Two things can result from talking and demonstrating locally. You become known and you can start building a list of names and addresses of prospective clients. There is also the opportunity to sell your work at local meetings with a percentage going to the organizers. Have cards to hand out to buyers or interested people who may become regular customers. With this system, one thing leads to another and you may even have to limit how often you go out on such public relations exercises.

Among the opportunities for beginners are local arts and crafts exhibitions. It seems every fund-raising body now has an 'exhibition' which is really an art/craft sale but not all of these are very selective or well displayed and organized. Some that have been established over a number of years have a good reputation but there are just as many of a poor standard. If you are invited to take part, check each one carefully beforehand. You will need to consider how far ahead you have been invited. Some organizations seem to think a month is sufficient advance warning. Is there a well organized committee providing properly printed information or is the invitation a casual phone call? Who is responsible for insurance, security and publicity? What space has been allocated to you and what expectations are demanded of you to attend?

When these fund-raising sales were new, the craftsperson was well looked after and one expected to work and help the charity which took only 20 per cent commission. The success of such enterprises had resulted in a proliferation of similar 'sales' and the commission is often more than 25 per cent. Often there is an entry fee to exhibit and if you attend opening night, even if it is to help and promote your work, you may be charged $6 to $10 for the privilege of the preview wine and cheese!

While these 'exhibitions' can offer good selling opportunities as the people who attend are there to spend and help their favourite charity, you will need to decide carefully which will help you most. So much poor work has flooded these sales that the whole system has harmed the serious artist and craftsperson by promoting poor quality and unrealistic pricing.

Local Shops

If local shops are handy to you, time and travelling expenses are cut down by selling to them. The type of shops to look for are boutiques selling clothing and jewellery, craft shops and gift shops. By looking in your area you will already have an understanding of the type of market for which the shops cater. The shop may be in a beach suburb where casual clothing is worn, or one which caters for tourists looking for souvenirs within a certain price range or it could be in a sophisticated business area with executives and trendy office employees as the customers. Analyse what type of work is sold in these shops and the prices being asked. When you approach retailers you will need to offer something appropriate but different from their normal stock.

Retailers will be looking for reliability and continuity of supply. If you are offering individual pieces say so, or if the pieces are one of a series, tell the retailer how many are in the range and how they vary.

If the work is a multiple production you must decide if it will be exclusive to that shop in that suburb.

Fashion and changing styles also need to be considered. Keep thinking ahead and do not expect to or be content to supply the same thing for months or years. The shop may change its range from summer to winter or may be altering its image such as moving into a lower price range to promote a faster turnover. The area may have gradually changed from a busy shopping centre to an office area. It is your responsibility to notice such changes and make your decisions.

Craft Shops

Every city and many large country towns have a few specialist craft shops which have a reputation for high quality craft which is exclusive to them. These shops are generally well suited for the tourist trade or in a busy, well populated part of town. The competition to have work accepted by these places may be tough but is worth the effort. Generally, jewellery is well displayed and taken care of—not put back with finger marks on it or the wrong way around. Your reputation can be enhanced by having your work in shops which have a good reputation.

Both specialist shops and local shops expect you to be reliable, able to supply on a regular basis, and keep ahead of the competition. To help you find these shops some of the State crafts councils have booklets listing galleries and craft shops. (See the Appendix.)

Markets

There are two kinds of market in this country, the occasional or regular street market and the specialized craft market.

An American idea that is catching on in Australia is the craft market. These are professionally organized and well planned, aimed at retailers in the first place and then open to the general public. Similar to trade fairs and often held in the same venues, the craft fairs are advertised in advance in city newspapers. The Crafts Council of Australia has initiated 'Craft Expo' trade fairs in Sydney and Melbourne. These have been held annually and have been a stunning success both financially and in exposing craftspeople to the trade and public. As the number of participants is limited, entry can be fairly competitive. Selection is sometimes by reputation and sometimes based on a presentation of work, so you need good current documentation.

The other type of market is one with stalls in the open or in community halls. These markets are advertised in local papers. In Sydney, as well as the long established permanent markets such as Paddy's and Paddington, nearly every suburb now seems to have a monthly market of its own. These markets are fast selling, well organized and charge a minimal stall fee. They are also fun. While this kind of market may not suit expensive silver jewellery it is a good place to sell low-cost items. This does not mean the standard of work is low, indeed much of it is high. There is generally not a lot of jewellery on display, mainly clothing, knick knacks, books and plants, so it is possible to get a good piece of the action. One more thought — if you have a stunning idea for a 'cheapie' — then hit the market with as much as you can on the one day. Next week, if it is as good as you thought, everyone else will be using your idea.

If you are going to use these outlets, look at them first to see what is selling and what you may need to set up a stall. You will need enough stock to keep going all day. Work out the sort of display you want and what you will need to set up. Generally, just a table which allows people to get close to the work is all that is needed, plus a mirror so they can see how the pieces look when worn. You will need a chair to sit down on during a lull, perhaps someone to keep you company and of course change and a money box.

When the day is over, no matter how tired you are, work out the money and check the number of pieces sold to see whether the venture was financially viable. List any feedback or comments you overheard. This will help you decide what stock to take next time.

Workshop Exhibitions

A selling exhibition held in your home or workshop needs at least six months' planning and considerable work beforehand. Make some decisions about the exhibition before you start. Will there be a theme or cohesive factor? Who do you expect to buy your jewellery? As you will be inviting previous customers, friends, and acquaintances you will have a good idea of what work is appealing and what prices people can afford.

1 Jewellery Work out how many pieces you may need and in what price range. Divide the number of pieces into rings, bracelets, neckpieces, brooches and objects. Have a list in your workshop and tick the pieces off as you complete them. Decide on some major pieces to add interest and variety and try to have a wide price range.

2 Timing Think carefully about the best time to hold the workshop exhibition. Before Christmas is the accepted spending period but there is also a lot of competition at that time. Early November is good before people become too busy with Christmas activities. Whenever you hold it, keep to the same dates each year so that people will remember and it becomes established.

3 Sharing If you have enough room, it is a good idea to invite another artist to join you. Combine with a painter or weaver or someone whose work will be displayed on the walls. Not only does it make a more colourful and interesting display but you can share costs, double the guest list and halve the work! Next year find someone new to share with and keep on adding to your guest list.

4 Invitations A guest list can be compiled from people you have already sold to, friends, friends of friends, neighbours, organizations you belong to, places you shop. Do not be shy about it. It is surprising how many people will want to come and feel flattered at receiving an invitation. It is embarrassing when acquaintances complain that they were not invited. Write on each invitation 'John and Mary and friends'. People will bring friends if you suggest it. Always carry a few spare invitations with you to give to people you happen to meet. Remember people are used to visiting homes, not galleries. They feel less formal and quite comfortable and can also visualize how a piece would look in their own home. Have more invitations printed than names on your list as you may find you'll need them.

It takes quite a long time to write on each invitation as well as address the envelopes. Aim to post them about two and a half weeks before the opening. This means the invitation arrives two weeks before the opening. Most people plan their outings that far ahead. If you post too early, people forget.

Two days is generally enough time for a workshop sale. Previous buyers, big spenders, really interested prospective buyers and a few friends who add sparkle should be selected from your invitation list to attend a 'preview' or 'opening night'. Allow enough space on the invitation to handwrite the details of date and time.

5 Display The actual arrangement of work is an art in itself. You must decide on all the display details, the materials to use, such as cloth, paper, cork, perspex, leaves, branches, driftwood, or whatever. Choose a background colour. Jewellery can often be well displayed against a strong background colour and it can help establish a solid theme with good overall visual impact. Vary the height of the display so everything is not on one level, flat on a table, but remember optimum viewing angles and positions. There are all sorts of ways to build an interesting display. Group various pieces like a still life but do not go overboard. Avoid clutter by making sure you leave space between your groups.

People like to handle and try on jewellery so you have to decide what to pin down and what to leave uncovered. I have always had everything easily available for handling without using display cases and I have never had a piece broken or taken. A mirror somewhere handy for people trying on work is necessary.

Setting up can take at least a day. Find a helpful friend, someone with a flair for arranging pieces and who does not mind hard work like moving furniture. If you need extra tables, then try planks on boxes from the greengrocer and cover them with material. Telephone books, styrene tomato boxes, all sorts of tricks can be used to vary height. Have some pot plants and greenery to fill odd corners.

6 Sales You will need a sales table and sales staff. Family and friends can help here. A sales system that is simple and quick is vital. I find a large cash book page with ruled columns works well. Have a column for item number and description, price, buyer's name and address, and if the piece had been taken or is to be collected or delivered and whether payment has been made. Exhibit 6-1 shows a sample page. If sales are brisk, two or more people can work at the business table, each with a separate sales sheet. This may sound cumbersome but once you start, it is efficient and also gives vital information for next year. I also have a chair for buyers to sit down which is useful when they want to write a cheque! You will need change for the cash buyers and it is easier to price items in round figures.

You need to decide if sales made on 'opening night' or at the 'preview' should be taken away by the purchaser or collected later. I put red spots on anything sold on the opening night. Quite often when buyers come back to collect their piece a day later, they will buy again. I wrap some of the red spot items and put them away next day. (See details under 'Next Day'.) You may already have specially designed packaging

Exhibit 6-1   Cash book entries

No.	Description	Price	Buyer's Name, Address	Taken/ Collect	Paid
6	Bracelet	$40	S. Winter, 36 High St, Endly	Taken	Pd
3	Weaving	90	F. Summer, 22 Tree Rd, Hay	To collect	To pay

or you may wish to consider something special like choosing coloured tissue to match your colour theme.

7 Opening night or preview This is when you need all the help that family and friends can give. It is an occasion so make it special with wine, cheese and soft drinks so people will relax and are more likely to buy. However, it is *not* a party—so don't let the wine flow too freely! If you are not sure how much wine you will need, your local liquor shop can tell you how many glasses to a flagon or bottle. They are also likely to have glasses you can borrow. Some shops will allow you to take extra bottles on a return basis if unopened. A reliable rule for quantity is two glasses per head and this adjusts so people who drink more compensate for those who drink less.

Everyone likes to talk to the craftsperson so you will need to avoid being tied down with one task or with one person. Your job is to circulate and speak to everyone. This is where family and friends act as staff for the sales table, as wine waiters, and for generally keeping an eye on things. Give each helper a specific job. Try not to go on too late as the next two days are liable to be busy with constant activity and you could then be working on your own.

8 Next Day Check the display by making sure it is all fresh and in place. Dust, remove ash, and check pieces for finger marks. Take away and wrap up any small, cheaper pieces that have been sold and put the buyer's name on the outside. It is a peculiar thing but invariably some people want the piece that is already sold and barely look at anything else. I put away almost everything that has been sold except the major works or focal pieces or work that has duplicates on display. A few red spots indicating sales do encourage people to buy.

Tidy the sales table, make new sales sheets ready for the day, sort out change and put away any cheques or bundles of notes.

A small but important detail to make note of is that your house number should be easily seen by day and night.

9 Closing When the exhibition closes, be quick and accurate in paying any fellow artists, returning borrowed equipment, delivering work to purchasers and balancing and banking the money. Later you can check the guest list to see who and how many came and if you have all their addresses. Go through the sales sheets and note for next year's preview or opening night, those who spent the most. I have a visitors' book that most people manage to sign. This provides a basis for next year's guest list.

10 Good advice Avoid taking orders unless you are very well organized and want to make such a piece or to please that particular person. You will be tired after such a hectic time and ready to relax. You will most likely be ready to go on to something new and will not need the pressure of unplanned deadlines.

This ten-point plan for a workshop or home selling exhibition is a good exercise to go through and can certainly be a moneymaking one.

Exhibition

I am using the word exhibition to describe a display of work at a gallery. The purpose may be to sell items exhibited, to display the results of a competition or perhaps to show collectors' items or pieces from specialized areas or overseas. Exhibiting one's work can be another opportunity for a jeweller to contact a different group of people, to become more widely known and to compare oneself with other jewellers.

An exhibition piece is often different from the steady selling pieces in that it attempts to be innovative, stimulating, exciting or shocking, show new directions, special techniques or new and unusual use of materials. Making exhibition pieces can therefore extend you technically and artistically. Having an exhibition, whether it's a one-man or a group show, is exciting and stimulating but hard work and exacting. You may not make a fortune, but an exhibition is something to aim for and include in your selling programme as it can broaden your market and enhance your reputation.

There are several types of galleries: public galleries such as national, State, regional, municipal and commercial galleries. Commercial galleries operate, in various ways:

- The gallery that has group or one-artist shows for a limited time and where the gallery owner/manager acts as your agent for the duration of the exhibition

- A gallery that will lease its space to artists
- A gallery that has a variety of work on consignment and operates almost as a shop but occasionally features one artist's work.

Whichever of these commercial galleries you exhibit in, you will need to be clear on the business arrangements. The important questions are:

- The percentage taken by the gallery
- When and how you will be paid
- What you are required to provide; documentation, artist's statement, etc.
- How long before opening is work to be delivered
- What the gallery provides
- Who is responsible for setting up the exhibition and taking it down again
- Freight and intransit insurance to and from the exhibition
- Who takes responsibility for invitations, their design, printing and postage, advertising, publicity, guest list, refreshment
- Insurance during the exhibition.

To clarify these questions, it is wise to work out a written contract with the gallery director. If the gallery does not already have a standard contract available, you can write a simple one yourself. An excellent example of a contract is in Shane Simpson's book *The Visual Artist and the Law*, published by The Law Book Company. This book is current, written for Australian conditions and will help you with any business agreements. Some Craft Councils now have a basic contract available for a few dollars.

Apart from business arrangements, there is other information the gallery will need for the catalogue and for their staff to discuss your work with the public. This will include a list of exhibits with descriptions or titles of works, dimensions and technical information and any display instructions. Documentation will need to include your biography and perhaps photographs and personal statement on your aims, methods and philosophy of work.

Sales Interviews

In the beginning before your work is known, you will need to make the initial contact with sales outlets such as boutiques and craft shops for an appointment and an interview. Be professional and organized in your approach and presentation as well as in your portfolio.

Before you make an appointment, find out as much as you can about the outlet you will be visiting. Some other craftsperson whose work is displayed may be able to help you. Have a close look at the operation, the space, the way work is displayed, the number of customers going in as well as comparing jewellery already in the shop with your own work. Next, make an appointment with the shop owner, manager or store buyer, making sure you know the person's name. Leave your phone number in case the appointment has to be cancelled, and if for any reason you have to change an appointment, give as much notice as possible and suggest another time.

When you keep the appointment, be on time and try to be confident and relaxed. Plan on the interview taking about half an hour and spend the first fifteen minutes presenting your portfolio and samples. Leave the rest of the time for discussion and answering questions as you can always ask the interviewer if she would like to see more samples later. Make packing your samples as simple and fast as possible, in soft bags, an easily opened case or even a soft material roll with pockets. It is all part of a professional approach.

When the interview is successful and the retailer would like to have your work in her shop, you will need to arrive at a business agreement, although a different one from that with galleries. You will most likely have to leave the work on consignment while the retailer sees what response there is from the public. (Consignment and wholesale selling are explained at the end of this chapter.) After dealing with the shop on a consignment basis and when you have established yourself as a regular supplier, try to make an outright sale to the retailer at a discount, generally 50 per cent off the retail price. If this is not acceptable, ask for a combination of the two. You must be clear about the price you want for each piece. Mark-up percentages vary and are set by the retailer. You could discuss this and indicate retail prices set for your work by other outlets. From the first interview, try to establish a pleasant working relationship. An interested retailer will promote your work, display it prominently and look after it carefully; and know how catches work or the variety of ways a piece may be worn. Any information which helps to sell your jewellery is to your mutual advantage. Try and obtain feedback on what sells quickly, at what price, and why. The retailer may be able to suggest new ideas and materials. The more a retailer understands your work and *how* you work, the more helpful she can be in ordering in advance and in quantity.

If you are not successful at an interview try not to be disappointed but find out *why*. It could be for simple reasons not connected with your work. If the buyer says there is too much stock at the moment or your work is not suitable for the shop, thank her and ask if you may call again. Do not lose heart from one knockback and do not take it personally as it is your work that is being evaluated, not you.

Success at one retail outlet will give you confidence to try others, but be selective. A shop with quality handcrafted and exclusive work is the type of place to look for. It is no use competing with mass-produced or similar manufactured jewellery, so carefully choose your outlets to suit your work. Increase the number of outlets slowly so that you do not have more orders than you can cope with. Retail outlets, above all, want a reliable supplier. It may not be wise to have your work in too many places in the same area. It is usually better to be selective and therefore more exclusive.

Consignment Selling

This entails leaving your work at a shop with an agreement that you will be paid only after the piece has been sold. It is unusual for shops to have a consignment agreement form available therefore it is wise business practice for you to provide one. A consignment agreement would include the name and address of the supplier (you) and the name and address of the retailer. Most important on the agreement would be the terms of payment and how soon payment should be made after each piece has been sold. The wholesale price of each piece should be clearly listed on the accompanying invoice. Insurance and damages should be discussed and written into the agreement. Both parties should sign and date the agreement. It is important that beginners make sure they understand the payment terms. One misunderstanding could be that payment would not be made until *all* work was sold.

There are disadvantages to consignment selling but we have little choice as not many craft shops are willing to buy outright. These disadvantages include not being paid on time and having to chase payment. Damage to work can cause another problem as the jeweller receives no compensation unless the shop has agreed to it beforehand. There is also more incentive for a retailer to sell work he owns rather than work that is on consignment. But there are some advantages to selling on consignment, mainly that, as a beginner, you have the chance of promoting yourself and your work and there is often the opportunity to display a wider variety of pieces. Another advantage is that you can withdraw your work from that outlet and put it in a special sale or place it elsewhere. Sometimes the commission on consignment work is lower than the wholesale price at which a retailer will purchase.

Wholesale

Once you establish yourself with a retailer, it may be possible to arrange to sell some work wholesale and to have some on consignment. If you receive a large order from a shop, I think it is only fair to receive a deposit with the written order and an agreement to be paid on delivery of the completed work. It is your time and materials that are being tied up and you cannot afford to subsidize other small businesses.

A written and numbered order is one way of making sure you will not be left with unwanted goods if the shop owner should have a change of mind.

There are reliable shops selling on consignment and a few buying wholesale from the craftsperson. You will inevitably learn by trial and error and eventually build your own network of reliable outlets.

Robyn Gordon

Robyn Gordon works full-time as a jeweller putting into practice many of the ideas in this book. After receiving her Diploma of Art Education and since doing her Graduate Diploma of Professional Art, Robyn converted from full-time teaching to making jewellery as her profession. Making jewellery was originally a by-product of her teaching and in the early stages Robyn did not think of herself as a jeweller. She makes pieces that are colourful, decorative, fashionable, and wearable, as well as distinctly Australian in theme. Her parrots, wildflowers, and Barrier Reef production pieces are as familiar as her iced vovos, licorice allsorts, and Luna Park series. The materials used are a collage of plastics, glass, mirror, manipulated fabrics, and a variety of natural and man-made 'found' materials. The most popular parrots and flowers are made from a thermo-setting plastic compound which is both resilient and flexible and can be mixed in a virtually limitless colour range which fires evenly and opaquely.

Working from home and managing her own business has meant developing a well defined work plan. Household tasks are shared with her husband and time together planned with safety valves of separate interests. Robyn finds she needs to be in the craft world and keep her contacts. The benefits of working at home mean problems can be solved as they occur and blocks of time for holidays can be arranged. A disadvantage of working at home is that work can get to be devouring and restrict other activities. Time is carefully planned. Robyn is responsible for design and fashion research as well as making the pieces. As jewellery has to go along with fashion, next season's colours and styles are taken into consideration.

Robyn is disciplined in the way she works, knowing what needs to be done, responding to pressure when necessary and working approximately the same number of hours each week. Nevertheless, her time is flexible and expands for interruptions. Planning includes time for record keeping although some professional advice is necessary in this area.

Selling has been carefully thought through from costing to selecting outlets and presentation. As Robyn's type of jewellery is labour-intensive the pricing of a new design is carefully monitored prior to marketing. She says 'The more I make the fast I get. If time runs and if I find I've speeded up I can adjust the price down from my original concept. Uneconomical lines are dropped or designs adapted slightly. When a price is arrived at, it is kept to. All work is sold outright and nothing on consignment.' Outlets are selected to be compatible with Robyn's work and there are a limited number in most Australian States and Territories. Special one-off pieces for exhibitions or individual items are more complex in detail but every piece is of the same high technical standard and thoroughly scrutinized.

Expansion in the future has been thought about and the decision made to keep the business at its current level to facilitate individual control of the market force. It also means Robyn is personally responsible for all the finished work and has only herself to monitor for quality control.

How did Robyn Gordon get started? Her work was included in a group show *'Project 33—ART CLOTHES',* during December 1980 to February 1981 and curated by Jane de Teliga at the Art Gallery of New South Wales. After this exhibition Robyn and Ruby Brilliant, a fibre craftsperson, approached Macquarie Galleries in Sydney with a selection of their work. Both went consciously to impress and present themselves professionally. Bravado is needed when approaching galleries! Since that initial exposure and first stunning exhibition, everyone comes to Robyn. Before that success, the elitist attitude of some galleries amazed, disappointed and angered Robyn. It needs perseverance and determination to be successful. Gallery shows are not a financial exercise but are necessary for exposure, and for establishing a reputation as a professional artist.

Robyn Gordon is using many different ways to sell her jewellery, all of them successful and used for their specific purpose.

CHAPTER 7

Managing Money

A HANDFUL of money! You've made your first sales and life looks golden. You are in business! Or are you?

How do you know you've made a profit or even covered costs? How did you arrive at a price for the pieces you made? Did you look at similar pieces in the market and then lower your prices? Was it an inspired guess? How do you know you will have enough money to buy more materials and tools?

It is quite simple to keep financial records, have a financial plan and know at what particular time you become financially secure. Money comes in and some money goes out. Making sure it does not all go out and that you hold on to a reasonable amount is what you will read about in this chapter. If you are going to be in business making jewellery, you need to develop some skills in money management. It is not difficult; everyone handles money, has some income and needs to budget and balance.

If you have been in the work force you will have received a regular wage. You will have planned to cover your commitments and perhaps will have managed to save some of your income. Managing a household is the same as running a business and we all have some expertise. Perhaps you have lived on a student allowance and learned to budget and carefully plan your expenditure. At any time you could tell how many cents you had in your purse. Each week you would know your fixed expenses; rent, food, fares. You would know how much you would need to spend on materials and clothes, and these may have had to be saved for until you had enough to buy them. All this is useful experience for a jeweller who is just starting out.

Having decided to be a self-supporting jeweller, it is important to separate the business expenses from your personal expenses. When making jewellery was a hobby you may not have kept a clear-cut line between the two. As an income-earning jeweller, you will need to keep clear records for pricing, to know how much you are earning, to know what profit you are making and for taxation. Whether you start in a small way or a grand way, it is vital to be able to price your work accurately, based on all your costs. Too often the wide difference in price between similar pieces of work is a result of the part-time craftsperson not depending upon it for a living, while the full-time person has to be realistic because his craft is his livelihood.

To understand how to keep records, let us look at the words used, and what information is needed. You may not be familiar with some of these terms but we all know the meaning of the word profit. It's what we're after!

Consignment This means leaving your work in a shop and not being paid for it until the work is sold. There are advantages and disadvantages in consignment, although for a beginner it is a good way to start selling.

When work is left on consignment you will need an *invoice* as shown in Exhibit 7–1, plus an agreement listing consignment conditions (see Chapter 6 on selling). Refer also to Shane Simpson's *The Visual Artist and The Law* for 'a standard agreement for the consignment of artworks'.

Exhibit 7–1   Invoice

No. 24	R. Stubbs	2.4.86
	131 Upside Street	
	BEACHSIDE 2101	
	Phone: 00076	

Supplied to:	Niki's Boutique	
on consignment:	Milsons Road	
	NORTH SYDNEY	

4 sterling silver rings @ $55		$220
2 silk and metal necklets @ $70		140
1 sterling silver chain $80		80
		$440

Discount This is the percentage taken off the recommended selling price to arrive at a wholesale price. If the retail price is halved, the discount is 50 per cent which is used when the jeweller wishes to set the retail price. The retailer would need to know what discount he would receive to arrive at a wholesale price.

Hourly rate You should be able to live on your wage the same as if you were working for someone else. What minimum wage would you expect to receive or alternatively what would you pay someone to do this work? A casual worker may get $5 per hour, a mechanic $16, a service repairman $25.

As a beginner, let us use $8 an hour as an example. How many hours a week can you work? If it is a full-time occupation in your own business you would expect to work fifty hours at a minimum. Fifty hours at $8 an hour would be $400. Would this be enough after tax to live on in the manner you would like to? If not, you must increase the number of hours worked, or the rate. This is the simplest way of working out hourly rate.

Labour These costs apply to the time and skill, both physical and mental, used in your business.

Mark-up This is the percentage added on to the wholesale price by the retailer. If the retailer doubles the wholesale price the mark up is 100 per cent.

Material cost The cost of the raw materials used. If you buy special material for one piece and only use part of it and cannot see a use for what is left, then the whole cost of that material is counted. It is possible to put a value on 'found' materials, such as shells, by comparing similar items sold in shops.

Overhead expenses These are all the expenses connected with running a business whether you are producing anything or not. Rent, electricity, gas, telephone, insurance, transport, accountant, professional expenses such as your membership in the Jewellers and Metalsmiths Group of Australia (JMGA), stationery, packaging and tool replacements.

If you have a home workshop some of these overheads will need to be worked out by taking a percentage of the household cost. A telephone is an easy example. If you think a quarter of the calls made are in connection with your work, then a quarter of the phone bill forms part of the overhead costs.

You can work out your overhead costs for twelve months, three months, monthly, or weekly. Suppose your overhead costs for one month total $20 and your material costs for one week are $80. Your overhead costs are a quarter of your material costs. So add $5 for overhead to the material costs of $80. This is a simple way of working out what to add on to each piece of work for overhead.

Another way to work out overhead is to divide the monthly overhead by the number of hours worked. Suppose the monthly overhead costs are $300 and the number of hours you will work for the month are 200. Therefore, you add $1.50 per hour for overhead costs to your other hourly costs.

You need to be able to go back and prove that the allowance for overhead actually covered your expenses.

Profit Profit is the money left over after all outgoings have been deducted from income. It is the return on the money invested in your business for the risks you take. Profit is important as it allows you to expand, buy new equipment and cover any losses.

Unless you add profit to your price you are just working for wages, that is, being paid for your labour.

Retail Price The amount charged by the person who sells to the consumer.

Sales tax Sales tax is calculated on the wholesale price. It is an indirect tax collected by manufacturers and some wholesalers on behalf of the government. There are many exemptions and different rates of sales tax. It is best to be advised on sales tax by applying to the Taxation Department in your State. Item 100 is the relevant one.

The Crafts Council of Australia has published an excellent and helpful pamphlet on sales tax.

Whole price The total cost of materials, plus labour, plus overhead plus profit. If you are paying sales tax, it is worked out on these.

Now you have the right words and terms you can make use of them. You can start to sort all those odd pieces of paper into a system. The papers you have will fall into two categories: information and financial.

Information

The most important information you need to keep track of is orders. Have an order book which includes all details: the date the order is taken, the date the work is needed, size, if applicable, and, of course, name, address and telephone number of the customer. If you have given a quote, make sure that is written down too.

Another essential is an accurate record of all your work which is out on consignment; who has it, a description of the pieces and the prices and the date you supplied the work, any payments received and calls to try and collect payment!

Information you will need to file includes suppliers, galleries, shops that sell jewellery, customer's names and addresses. A heap of mail will keep on filling your letterbox, invitations, craft shows and competitions, newsletters. Throw out what is not current and survive the paper war.

What is most necessary is a good diary near the telephone and an easily read calendar. A planning calendar is handy; it is incredible how deadlines are suddenly there.

Manila folders, a file drawer or box, diary, calendar and notebook will all help to keep the information sorted out and easily accessible.

Financial Records

A simple way of keeping a financial record is to have an account book with ruled columns. On one side you write all the money coming in (receipts) and on the other side all the money going out (payments). This is your day book and you should write down any transactions the day they happen. It is so easy to forget to enter an item the next day. Exhibit 7-2 shows a sample sheet.

On the receipts' side you show the date, who paid and what for, the amount received and whether it was by cash or cheque, and the receipt number.

The payments' side will show who was paid and what for, the amount paid and whether by cash or cheque. If by cheque show the cheque number.

This is simple book-keeping. Write legibly and include all the information. Later an accountant may need to check your books, and personal shorthand and jotted notes are of no use to him and may even cost you money for his time lost reading the figures the wrong way.

Talk to an accountant if you are unsure of how to set out your books. It is a good idea to build a

Exhibit 7–2 Example of day book

Receipts		$	Payments			$
May 8	Sterling ring cheque J. Strong	70	May 8	leather belting	cash	8
				silk	cash	15
May 24	Niki's Boutique cheque as per invoice No.24	350	May 10	Stainless steel tube cheque No. 271654		25
			May 26	telephone share of account cheque No.271.655		70
May 31		$420	May 31			$128

reasonable working relationship with your accountant from the beginning. If you are in doubt about anything or run into financial problems your accountant can advise you. He may be the accountant at your bank or a privately practising accountant who specializes in small businesses.

Another reason to develop a good understanding with your accountant is that once a year at income tax time you will need to have your books checked and your tax returns prepared. No one likes paying more tax than he has to and a skilful accountant will save you money. An accountant will know what you can claim as expenses, how to value your stock at its lowest value and how to depreciate equipment.

Many small businesses fail in the first two years. The reasons are not for lack of hard work or enthusiasm but more for failing to understand the financial side, and that the aim of all this hard work is profit. With your accountant's help and advice make sure you understand keeping financial records and how to read a simple balance sheet.

A simple balance sheet lists all your assets on one side and all your liabilities on the other. Assets are all the things you own such as materials, tools, finished pieces, plus money owed to you. Liabilities are what you owe, such as money to the bank, unpaid bills, or suppliers for materials. The excess of what you own—your assets, over what you owe—your liabilities, is your equity in the business.

Beware of an excess the other way around, that is liabilities over assets. If that happens you are bankrupt! If you do a simple balance sheet once a month, any increase in your equity is your profit. A sample balance sheet is shown in Exhibit 7-3

When establishing your business it is advisable to do a balance sheet once a month. It is vital to know that you are making a profit. Keeping a close watch on profit, or even a loss one month, will save you from being one of the small businesses that fail for lack of financial understanding.

With continued profit you can invest in more tools, improve your output, bring prices down on some items and ultimately benefit the consumer. With lower prices and a higher volume I can see every person, man or women, adult or child using jewellery as an everyday necessity. Imagine the time when everyone chooses which piece of jewellery to wear each day, the way we choose which shoes to put on.

Let us sum up the main financial aspects to keep in mind.

Exhibit 7–3 Example of balance sheet as at 31.3.86

Assets		Liabilities	
Petty cash	100	Owed to suppliers	50
Bank balance	300	Expenses yet to pay	120
Consignment	600	Bank loan	300
Stock materials	350		470
pieces	300		
Tools	2 000	Net worth	3 240
Expenses forward paid	60		
(telephone rent)			
	3 710		3 710

Net worth in March	$3 710
Net worth in Feb.	$3 660
	$50
Plus paid to self	$400
Profit	$450

- **Profit** More money coming in than going out.
- **Receipts and Payments** What money is coming in and what money is being spent or going out.
- **Balance Sheet** A list of your assets and liabilities. The excess of assets over liabilities is your equity in the business and any increase in equity is profit.
- **Labour** Am I being paid enough for what I do?

Pricing

Many crafts people, particularly jewellers, have difficulty in pricing their work. Whenever beginners get together the conversation inevitably turns to 'How do you price your work?' It is a very simple process once you learn the formula. What makes it difficult for beginners is personal involvement. Half the people feel so strongly about their creative input that whatever the price is, it will not be enough. The other half feel so modest that they do not count their creativity at all. Neither of these feelings have anything to do with the real value.

Whether you are a part-time jeweller or making jewellery as a leisure occupation, you must be realistic in pricing. It is fine to be competitive but most unfair to the full-time craft jeweller who is trying to earn a living. If the part-timer undercuts prices greatly, it makes the full-time professional look expensive. It also makes it difficult for those part-timers who move into full-time production and need to increase their prices.

There are several ways to price your work. The first is by directly analysing all the costs in producing a particular piece as shown opposite in Exhibit 7-4.

As you can see from the sample the outlets that only mark up 40 per cent to 60 per cent should be able to sell your work and keep it moving quickly. If you can find these outlets, concentrate on selling your work through them.

Some crafts people include a design fee in their costs. This is to cover their expertise and the years spent in acquiring it. The design fee can be a flat rate per piece or a fee of so many dollars per day.

The second way of pricing is by comparison. What is the price of a similar item on the market? Have

Exhibit 7–4 Analysis of costs

Materials	$80
Labour 4 hours @ $15	60
Overhead (¼ material cost)	20
Desired profit 20% of costs	32
	$192

Therefore the wholesale price is	$192
If paying sales tax it would be calculated on this.	
Retail price with 100% mark up	$384
If consignment mark up is 50%	$288

a look in all jewellery outlets. Ask yourself would you pay that price for the piece? Comparative pricing is a very good indication of what the market will bear. You will still need to be aware of production costs so that you can backtrack and see if the price is reasonable. Ask yourself, 'Am I making any money if I sell at a similar price?' Would I have to lower my labour rate or profit percentage to match this price?

What if the price is too high whichever way you work it out? What can you do? The first area to look at is the design. See if the piece can be simplified in the number of processes used. It may be necessary to go over each process several times until you have arrived at a solution that will be more suitable for a production piece.

Look at each of the costs and see whether you can cut down in any particular area.

Materials Are you buying as cheaply as possible, are you using them carefully and getting the most out of them? Perhaps alternative, cheaper materials could be used just as effectively.

Labour Perhaps you are not very skilful yet. The more pieces you make, the faster you will become so it is partly a matter of practice. Is your time being used efficiently so you are doing all the same processes at the one time, for example, soldering. It could be that one process needs a machine tool rather than a hand-tool.

Overheads Where can you cut down on overhead costs? Check that you worked out correctly the telephone, rent and power percentage if you are working at home. See if packaging could be simpler. Look at each part of overhead to see where savings can be made.

A longer production run could even be the answer as this could spread the costs over a greater number of pieces.

There are some areas you should not change. Safety is one and quality another. Do not be tempted to increase the number of orders to the extreme pressure point. It will soon show in the quality of your work as you will be tempted to compromise on workman-ship. Increased orders and pressure could also mean late deliveries. Your reputation will suffer from poor workmanship and delayed deadlines. Then you will have difficulty in selling and getting new orders.

One way of keeping prices down is to spread the costs. This is called 'averaging'. Some items that you can make cheaply and quickly sell easily at a high price and higher profit. This profit can be used to offset a lower profit on labour intensive items. An example is a small sterling silver ring band. These are sold widely for $6 to $10. The wholesale price is a fraction of this as they can be made quickly and easily. There is no point in selling these rings for $3. The buyer will query whether the material is really sterling silver, so you may as well have the higher profit. This will allow you to cut the price of a more complicated piece down to an acceptable market price without making a loss.

Other considerations in pricing are rather nebulous as they depend on fashion, the area where you live, where you are selling, who you are selling to and why the work is being bought. This is really the psychology of pricing. Jewellery is generally priced in round figures, $100, $5, not like supermarkets that scream $99.00 or $4.90. Somehow, the round figure seems to indicate quality. Another peculiarity is that people expect to pay over a certain price for some things. Think of a plain wedding ring not very different from the sterling silver bands in the example above, but a great price jump away. So social reasons play a part in pricing.

Handmade jewellery can also be a status symbol regardless of the value of the piece. Some people like to wear jewellery that is recognizable as being made by a well known jeweller.

Craft generally is on the upswing and for people who like to be individual, handmade jewellery is an obvious choice.

APPENDIX X

Information and Sources of Supply

INFORMATION for the craftsperson can become a flood of paper easy to sink under, time-consuming to wade through but, like water, necessary to life. To help you find the most useful sources, I have listed them under three main headings: organizations, courses, publications.

Organizations

First and foremost is:

Jewellers and Metalsmiths Group of Australia
c/- Craft Council of Queensland
109 Edward Street
Brisbane, 4000.

This is the Australia-wide craft jewellers and metal-smiths organization that was formed in January 1981.

If you are serious about your work it is a must. They publish an informative monthly newsletter, *Lemel*, which has articles on exhibitions, competitions, technology, suppliers and overseas events. Every two years JMGA holds a three to four day conference with speakers, demonstrations and many opportunities to talk shop with other jewellers.

State Jewellers Groups

Some States have strong working groups which have been established for a long time. Other States have newer groups that are independent of the JMGA but keep in close contact. JMGA or the Crafts Council in your State can give you the name and address of the current Secretary of the following:

- West Australian Jewellers Group
- Adelaide Jewellery Group
- Darwin Jewellers Group
- Sydney Jewellers Group
- Queensland Jewellery Workshop Group

Craft Council of Australia

100 George Street, The Rocks, NSW 2000.
As the coordinating body for the State Crafts Councils, the Craft Council of Australia represents Australia on the World Crafts Council. It is a non-governmental body partly funded by the Crafts Board of the Australia Council. CCA comprises the administration, projects office, crafts resource productions and *Craft Australia*. Its activities include the *Crafts Register* which lists biographical details of Australian craftspeople and can

be used for commissions, sales, exhibitions and research. Through Craft Resource Productions, it publishes a range of pamphlets, books and directories on all aspects of craft. An information service provides information on the crafts in Australia and overseas.

State Crafts Council

Basically the aims of the State crafts councils are to coordinate craft activities within the State, to be a communication and information centre and to encourage appreciation of the crafts. Each State has a different range of activities including specialist workshops, lectures, exhibitions, slide kit hire, service and newsletters. Their locations are:

Australian Capital Territory
   1 Aspinal Street, Watson, 2602

New South Wales
100 George Street, The Rocks, 2000.
Northern Territory
Conacher Street, Bullocky Point, Darwin, 5794.
Queensland
   109 Edward Street, Brisbane, 4000.

South Australia
   169 Payneham Road, St Peters, 5069

Tasmania
   77 Salamanca Place, Hobart, 7000.

Victoria
   7 Blackwood Street, North Melbourne, 3051.

Western Australia
   76 Newcastle Street, Perth, 6001.

The Crafts Board of the Australian Council

PO Box 302, North Sydney 2060.
Grants are available to assist craftspeople in several areas such as workshop development, crafts training in production and workshop management, and traineeships. A booklet with conditions and full details on how to apply for grants is published annually and is available from the Crafts Board.

Local Arts and Crafts Societies

A list of these is generally available from your State Crafts Council. Local groups are useful for putting you in touch with other jewellers and crafts people in your area and advising you of local opportunities such as classes, exhibitions, craft competitions and selling outlets. Some State art galleries have a list of art and craft societies and local councils which hold annual competitions with substantial prizes.

Community Arts Programmes

Many local councils now have community arts officers who should be a fund of information on what is happening in your area. Community arts centres where you can learn or teach, exhibitions and competitions and lists of appropriate local organizations are all part of the community arts officers' responsibility. Some municipalities may even want a mayoral chain or special piece for a visiting dignitary, so get to know your community arts officer.

Courses

There are so many opportunities to learn how to make jewellery that you should be able to find one to suit you. There are full-time or part-time courses, degree, diploma, or certificate courses, college courses, technical colleges, evening schools and private teachers.

New South Wales

Sydney College of the Arts, Balmain
Riverina College of the Arts, Wagga Wagga
City Art Institute, Sydney
College of Technical and Further Education, Randwick

Victoria

Royal Melbourne Institute of Technology, Melbourne
Melbourne College of Advanced Education, Melbourne
Chisholm Institute of Technology, Frankston
Victoria College, Burwood
College of Technical and Further Education, Collingwood

Queensland

Brisbane College, Seven Hills
Brisbane College, Kelvin Grove

South Australia

South Australia College of Education, Adelaide

Western Australia

Western Australia Institute of Technology, Perth

Tasmania

Technical College of Advanced Education, Launceston

Australian Capital Territory

Canberra School of Art, Canberra

Evening colleges, private teachers, craft workshops, and community learning centres generally advertise classes at the beginning of each term with some courses quite comprehensive and others for the hobby or leisure-time student. State crafts councils and community arts officers will know what is available in your suburb or town.

Publications

As a compulsive reader I could spend a fortune on books and magazines. Every week I find something new and interesting. Magazines, newsletters, catalogues, serious books and glossy coffee table books are in constant supply. To save you a fortune and a lot of time, here is a list of those I enjoy. Find them at the library, buy some, or arrange to exchange with a friend.

Periodicals

American Craft, bi-monthly of the American Crafts Council, Membership Department, PO Box 1308–CL, Fort Lee, New Jersey, NJ 02024, $US31.50.

Craft Australia, published quarterly by the Crafts Council of Australia, $22.50 a year.

Craft N.S.W., bi-monthly newsletter of the Crafts Council of NSW. Each State Crafts Council publishes its own newsletter which is included in the membership fee. Contact the Crafts Council in your State.

Crafts, published six times a year by the British Crafts Council, 8 Waterloo Place, London, SW1 Y4AT, £11.50 a year, including postage.

European Jeweller, monthly magazine published by Ruhle-Diebener-Verlag, GmbH & Co. KG, PO Box 250, D–7000 Stuttgart 70. No English translation, written in German.

Lemel, monthly newsletter of the Jewellers and Metalsmiths Group of Australia. Membership includes the newsletter.

Metalsmith, quarterly of the Society of North American Goldsmiths, Dept OM, 2849 St Ann Drive, Green Bay, Wisconsin, WI54301, $US30, a year, plus postage.

Ornament, a quarterly of Jewelry and Personal Adornment, POB 35029, Los Angeles, California CA90035-0029, $US22.

For your health's sake, it would be prudent to check back on Martha Henderson's article, 'The Health Hazards of Silver Soldering' in *Craft NSW Magazine*, No.152, October, 1983.

Books

Listed below are reference manuals for your workshop.

Centrifugal or Lost Wax Jewelry Casting, by Murray Bovin, first published in 1970 by Murray Bovin, New York, thoroughly explains the processes of casting and has many useful black and white photographs.

Contemporary Jewelry, by Phillip Morton, first published in 1970 and revised in 1976 by Holt, Rinehart and Winston in New York is an attractive, well illustrated, easy to read book covering many aspects of jewellery including history, design, marketing and production.

Metal Techniques for Craftsmen, by Oppi Untracht, first published in 1969, and revised in 1972 by Robert Hale & Co. in London, is a basic manual on the methods of forming and decorating metals. It is an excellent workshop reference book which most jewellers would make their first choice.

Jewelry, Concepts and Technology, by Oppi Untracht, published by Doubleday & Co New York in September, 1982. It is as useful and thorough as Oppi Untracht's other book.

The Design and Creation of Jewellery, by Robert von Neumann, first published in 1962, and revised in 1973 by Pitman in London is a fine textbook for the beginner with easily understood explanations of basic techniques, as well as more complicated processes such as granulation and mokume.

Listed below are books that are not reference manuals but nevertheless are useful as well as pleasurable as it's nice to know what the rest of the world is making in jewellery.

Body Jewellery. Donald Wilcox, published in 1974 by Pitman in London.

Contemporary Jewelry. A Critical Assessment 1945–1975, Ralph Turner, published in 1976 by Studio Vista in London.

Metal Jewelry Techniques, by Marcia Chamberlain, published in 1976, by Pitman, London.

Do not limit yourself to books on jewellery. Look into design, plastics, leather, textiles and body decoration. Resource Productions, Crafts Council of Australia, has issued *Books on Metal/Jewellery, a descriptive bibliography,* 1981. This publication lists books on jewellery, metalsmithing, materials, tools and tool making, techniques and related areas such as gems. The books were selected and annotated by leading Australian craftspeople and will help the experienced jeweller, the beginner, student, teacher and librarian.

Supply Sources for Tools and Materials

The Crafts Council of each State has compiled lists of supply sources and these have been published in 1982 by the Crafts Resource Productions of the Crafts Council of Australia in six booklets, one for each State as *A Guide to Craft Supplies.*

These booklets list the craft suppliers for each State under media headings, plus book suppliers, craft groups and organizations. These booklets are available from the State Craft Councils.

The New South Wales and Victoria booklets could be helpful no matter what State you live in and it's advisable to have one of these two as well as your own State booklet.

New South Wales additional sources are:

A. & G. Precision Engineering Co.,
   1 Dale Street,
   Brookvale.
   Jewellery stamps for metal made to order.

Artistcare (Letraset House),
   346 Kent Street,
   Sydney
   Artist/designer supplies including wet medium acetate.

Atlas Steels (Australia) Pty Ltd,
   23 Christina Road,
   Villawood.
   Stainless steel tube already annealled.

Bulgin Pty Ltd,
   129 Buckland Street,
   Alexandria.
   Welding products, extremely helpful.

Eastway Wireworks,
   84 Abercrombie Street,
   Chippendale.
   Brass, wire, mesh, stainless steel wire and mesh.

F. X. Plastics,
   77 Sydenham Road,
   Marrickville.

Fishermans World Sports Store,
   195 Hay Street,
   Sydney.
   Stainless steel trace wire and braided wire.

Gunz, Rudolf & Co. Pty Ltd,
   63 Ann Street,
   Surry Hills.
   All casting equipment, waxes, flexible shaft and motor, stainless steel wire (fine), drills, etc.

Hobbyco Pty Ltd,
    561 George Street,
    Sydney.

Jenssens Watchmakers Supplies,
    9 York Street,
    Sydney.

Lawrence Smith & Canning Pty Ltd,
    27 Leslie Street,
    Lakemba.
    Rouge, tripoli, buffs, auflux.

McPhersons Ltd,
    205 Euston Road,
    Alexandria.
    Metals and tools.

Selby's Scientific Ltd,
    61 Epping Road,
    North Ryde.
    Scales, handpieces, torches, mortar and pestle.

Stainless Steel Bar Co. Pty Ltd,
    Unit B, 349 Lyons Road,
    Five Dock.
    Angles, rod, section.

43A Higginbotham Road,
    Gladesville.
    Tubing.

Electronic supply shops are located in most suburbs as well as at the southern end of York Street, Sydney, for a specialized range of components.

South Australia additional sources are:

Eagle and Globe Steel,
    36 Hawker Street,

Brompton, 5007.
Specialized steels and metals.

Teuco Hobby,
18 Amanda Street,
Salisbury.
A variety of brass, copper and aluminium tube.

Universal Meyer,
282-294 Wright Street,
Adelaide.
Small nuts and screws.

Davison Lapidary,
96 Henley Beach Road,
Mile End.
Findings and boxes.

Western Australia additional sources are:

Gemrock Enterprises,
207 Murray Street,
Perth.
Stones cut to order.

Rudolf Gunz,
268 Peir Street,
Perth.
Casting supplies, burrs.

Soklich Trading Co.,
Dale Place,
Orange Grove.
Rocks and precious stones.

BIBLIOGRAPHY

Albrecht, Kurt, *Nineteenth Century Australian Gold and Silver Smiths,* 1969, Hutchison, Melbourne.

Brunel, Francis, *Jewellery of India. Five Thousand Years of Tradition,* 1972, National Book Trust, India, Iata Press Ltd, Bombay.

Hawkins, John, *Australian Silver 1800-1900,* 1973, National Trust of Australia, Sydney.

Keighery, Victoria, (compiler), *The Bumper Book of Craft Info: NSW,* Crafts Council of NSW, updated and published annually.

Larsen, Helge, (cataloguer), *Contemporary Australian Jewellery. Objects to Human Scale, 1980,* catalogue of the exhibition selected to tour Japan and some Southeast Asian countries, Reine Publishing, Japan.

Marquand, (editor), *How to Prepare Your Portfolio. A Guide for Students and Professionals,* 1981, Art Direction Book Company, New York.

Metcalf, Bruce, *'Techniques for the Head',* Metalsmith Magazine, Winter, 1983.

Morton, Philip, *Contemporary Jewelry,* 1970, revised 1976, Holt, Reinhart and Winston, New York.

New South Wales Women's Advisory Council to the Premier-, *Occupation: Housewife,* 1980, a discussion paper.

Resource Centre, Crafts Council of Australia, *Making It: A Business Guide for Craftsmen,* 1977.

Richards, Dick of the Art Gallery of South Australia, *Australian Jewellery. European Tour. 1982-1983,* Stock Journal Publishers and Advance Bookbinders.

Scott, Michael, *Crafts Business Encyclopedia,* 1977, Harcourt, Brace, Jovanich, New York.

Simpson, Shane, *The Visual Artist and the Law,* 1982, The Law Book Company, Sydney.

Spectrum Research for the Crafts Council of Victoria, *Australian Handcrafts Marketing and Communications Strategy Development,* 1980.

Wettlaufer, George and Nancy, *The Craftsman's Survival Manual. Making a full time or part time living from your craft,* 1974, Prentice-Hall, New Jersey.

Wilco, Donald, *Body Jewellery. International Perspectives,* 1974, Pitman, London.